MW00415309

The Interaction Field

The Revolutionary New Way to Create Shared
Value for Businesses, Customers, and Society

Erich Joachimsthaler

PUBLICAFFAIRS

New York

PublicAffairs
Hachette Book Group
1290 Avenue of the Americas, New York, NY 10104
www.publicaffairsbooks.com
@Public_Affairs

Printed in the United States of America

First Edition: September 2020

Published by PublicAffairs, an imprint of Perseus Books, LLC, a subsidiary of Hachette Book Group, Inc. The PublicAffairs name and logo is a trademark of the Hachette Book Group.

The publisher is not responsible for websites (or their content) that are not owned by the publisher.

Print book interior design by Amy Quinn.

Library of Congress Cataloging-in-Publication
Data Names: Joachimsthaler, Erich, 1956– author.
Title: The interaction field : the revolutionary new way to create shared
  value for businesses, customers, and society / Erich Joachimsthaler.
Description: First edition. | New York : PublicAffairs, 2020. | Includes
  bibliographical references and index.
Identifiers: LCCN 2020003216 | ISBN 9781541730519 (hardcover) | ISBN
  9781541730526 (ebook)
Subjects: LCSH: Social responsibility of business. | Consumer satisfaction.
  | Customer relations.
Classification: LCC HD60 .J63 2020 | DDC 658.4/06—dc23

LC record available at https://lccn.loc.gov/2020003216ISBNs: 978-1-5417-3051-9 (hardcover), 978-1-5417-3052-6 (ebook)

LSC-C

10 9 8 7 6 5 4 3 2 1

Contents

Introduction

For most of my career, which spans four decades, the conventional wisdom about a company's ability to create value was that it comes in the form of competitive advantage, differentiation, and growth, usually evaluated in terms of tangible assets, revenue, and profit.

In today's digital age—characterized not only by networks but by data-driven technologies, including artificial intelligence (AI), machine learning, and, soon, quantum computing—we have to think differently about how businesses create value.

The "interaction field" describes a new phenomenon that is just emerging and can be glimpsed in a handful of wildly successful companies such as Alibaba, Apple, Netflix, Google, and Amazon. It can also be found in some traditional businesses, from farming to fashion.

Interaction field companies thrive on the participation in value creation by many different groups: the company itself, its customers, suppliers, partners, and other stakeholders—as well as other entities you might not expect to see in the mix, such as competitors, observers, independent researchers, and government agencies.

By participating in these interconnected groups, interaction field companies can achieve a kind of unstoppable momentum and wild expansion that I call "velocity." It is a new form of multidimensional, constantly accelerating, explosive and smart growth that goes far beyond the traditional measures of sales increase, profit, or market capitalization.

Velocity sounds complicated, perhaps, but nothing's uncomplicated in this era of disruption, so let me simplify it with a metaphor. If you live in

New York City, as I do, you quickly learn about the power of velocity just from trying to get around town. If you step out of a taxi on the wrong side of the car at the wrong moment, for example, you may step into the path of an oncoming bus and be killed instantly. Get out the other side, and you risk an early demise from a bicyclist bombing toward you at top speed.

Now, that seems counterintuitive. A bike and a rider can be just as deadly as a loaded bus that weighs ten tons or more? For sure. The bus gets you with mass. The bike gets you with velocity. Most traditional companies are like a fully loaded bus. They thrive by creating enormous scale and assets, huge distribution networks, technology infrastructure, and big brands and reputations.

But then along comes a bike-like rival that has very little mass, doesn't care much about conventional practices in the business, and has a much smaller center but enormous velocity—it either rushes past its competitors or mows them down.

The traditional company is like BASF, Deutsche Bank, Siemens, or Volkswagen in Germany; or GE, General Motors, or Procter & Gamble in the United States; or Santander, Iberdrola, or Telefónica in Spain. These companies are the incumbent leaders in their industries. They run well-oiled, well-optimized value chains or pipeline businesses.

Consider a simple comparison between a traditional restaurant (the bus) and a food delivery business (the bike). In New York, a fine-dining restaurant is a combination factory, retail shop, and service provider. It costs about $300,000 to open a relatively small café or fast-casual restaurant in New York, and up to $10 million to set up a four-star establishment. Whatever form it takes, the restaurant will be dealing with fixed costs, professional fees for interior design and identity materials, a long-term lease or mortgage, depreciating assets such as ovens and food-processing equipment, and, of course, administrative staff, kitchen employees, and waitstaff.

Contrast the restaurant business with a food delivery service such as Seamless, Postmates, Uber Eats, or the UK-based Deliveroo. They are solving essentially the same customer problem that the fixed-cost restaurant is: What am I going to eat and when? But these delivery services present a very different solution. They feature a number of food and meal providers on their app and take what is essentially a royalty on every order they deliver, typically in the range of 20 to 30 percent of the order value. For the most part, they don't actually prepare the meals, so their costs are much lower than what's required to open and run a restaurant. The operators do not have to purchase perishable foodstuffs. They don't sweat out the long grueling hours. They don't even have to hire or manage kitchen staff or servers. For delivery, they rely on a small army of cyclists, but don't pay them a salary or benefits. Like Uber drivers, the bikers are free-lancers who get paid a commission for every order delivered.

Delivery companies can grow exponentially, from nothing to hundreds of thousands of daily users in a short period of time. Deliveroo, in fact, is the fastest-growing technology company in the United Kingdom. Just six years after founding, the company brings in over $600 million in annual revenue. And, of course, it is considered a unicorn start-up, with a market valuation of more than $2 billion. Deliveroo has rushed past some of the hottest restaurant chains, such as Shake Shack, and brings in twice the revenue.

Velocity—multidimensional, constantly accelerating, explosive and smart growth—is what all companies must strive for today, no matter their size or how long they've been in business. It doesn't matter whether the company is a start-up or an incumbent, a leading firm in an existing industry or part of a new and emerging category. So many of the business areas where traditional companies operate are being disrupted, disaggregated, and demolished by changing consumer habits, escalating customer expectations, and the effects of technology. The old business models cannot withstand or survive the torsion of these forces, but the new interaction field companies feed on them.

This kind of velocity is fueled by interactions. The more interactions a company can create among its participants, and the higher the quality or value of those interactions, the greater the velocity. As velocity increases, three things happen.

First, network effects kick in, which means that the product or service on offer becomes more valuable as more people contribute to it. Think

Airbnb. The more Londoners offer their spare rooms or stately homes or canal barges to travelers through Airbnb, the more valuable the service becomes—greater selection, increased availability, more variety and choices.

Second is virality. As people find value in a business offering, they voluntarily become advocates for it and encourage others to join. When Joshua and John Hanlon were fifteen and seventeen years old, they started a LEGO YouTube channel, *Beyond the Brick*, featuring builders from around the world and their amazing LEGO creations. Today, the channel has over 530,000 subscribers and over 200 million views. *Beyond the Brick* has gone viral to the benefit of both LEGO and the channel's users. It's informative, exciting, attractive, compelling—LEGO people want to join up, contribute, share videos, and talk about what they've experienced.

Third, as the company applies human knowledge and artificial intelligence to the large amounts of data being collected in the interactions, a learning effect emerges. That is, the more information the product gathers and synthesizes, the more valuable it becomes. Tesla collects more data through sensors and cameras than other manufacturers, which enables machine learning in its autopilot software, which increases driver safety. Teslas get smarter as you drive them, and the more Tesla drivers there are, the smarter the cars become.

After researching these companies and several hundred more, I've concluded that none has fully captured the opportunities of an interaction field company. Airbnb has a long way to go in terms of creating learning effects, for example. LEGO and Tesla are just at the beginning of leveraging the all-important network effect.

When a company takes advantage of these three effects, velocity intensifies, the effects build on each other and reinforce one another, and a virtuous cycle is created, which further fuels growth and ensures sustainability. As the cycle grows stronger and stronger, the value created can explode. So much so that the company is able to create shared value for everyone in the interaction field, well above and beyond the benefits it brings to its direct users.

I'm here to tell you why the velocity created by interaction field companies is the most important business model to emerge. It is absolutely essential that traditional firms, incumbents, and start-ups build their competitive advantage on this model. There is not another one that can address today's massive and widespread shifts in consumer habits and rise in customer expectations.

It does not matter whether you are selling retail, wholesale, or online from the basement of your home. It makes no difference if you sell forklifts, elevator systems, or megatons of soybeans to China. You may provide dental services in your neighborhood or accounting services to small businesses in your city. The shifts in consumer habits have impacted every industry and category.

One dominant change is sometimes referred to as the *Amazon Effect*. It originated with Amazon's offer, some fifteen years ago, of free shipping on orders of $25 or more. That evolved into Amazon Prime, the subscription service that features free shipping (included in the fee) and two-day delivery. Same-day shipping followed, which turned into free delivery within a two-hour window, and then one-hour same-day shipping with a single click. Not only did Amazon Prime attract millions more customers, it encouraged customers to purchase many more items than they previously had. Amazon Prime has elevated expectations about customer service, such that a merely good experience can easily get you two stars and a bunch of online complaints.

No matter what customers buy today, they want everything at the speed of Amazon, with the accuracy of a Google search result, the ease and zero-click convenience of a Domino's pizza order, the everyday low prices of Walmart, the personalization of Netflix, the charm of Singapore Airlines, and the availability and selection of Alibaba—whether they are purchasing a complex piece of medical equipment of a pair of sneakers.

Customers want companies to be responsive and human, socially responsible and environmentally aware. They want innovation and delight delivered to a world-class standard. They want security and privacy, as well as openness and transparency. They want the feel of a small local business with the capabilities of a global giant. A good share price would be nice, too, not to mention leaders that don't get thrown in jail or jettisoned for fraud or bad behavior.

Quite a challenge! It may sound ambitious, and it is. But I'm convinced it is the best, indeed the only, way forward for businesses today.

Living in New York, I have learned that one can get glimpses of the future before it arrives. I have seen the buses and I've experienced the bikes, and I know that velocity is what success will look like.

chapter one

The Interaction Field Model

How to Create Unstoppable Velocity

Before we explore the velocity phenomenon—what it is and how an enterprise, whether an incumbent or a start-up, can create, build, nurture, and maintain an interaction field that generates velocity—I need to briefly sketch out the two other standard approaches to value creation in business: the value chain and the platform.

The value-chain company is the classic, asset-heavy organization. It is structured as a hierarchy and has organized its key activities along the value chain from sourcing to design, manufacturing, marketing, and sales. Value is created through these activities and flows from the producer or company to the consumer. It has been the business model of the twentieth century and is like the fully loaded bus in New York traffic. In this kind of company, management wants to beat the competition and dominate an industry. They compete by accumulating and building assets and controlling them. They manage and optimize the pipeline—or a linear set of activities along the value chain—to target customers within well-defined industry or category boundaries, sell more to them, and maximize the experience curve, which means lower unit costs as production volume goes up. The value-chain company is a win-lose,

zero-sum-mind-set operation. Success is measured in terms of brand equity, market share, cost reduction, profit per customer, return on equity,
process speed, and a thousand other quantitative measures you'll find at
the back of the annual report. A value-chain company holds itself ac-
countable primarily to its shareholders and investors.

While the value-chain model has many advantages (control and sta-
bility chief among them) there are also many drawbacks. It is a model
that only scales linearly, leaves companies slow to innovate, requires assets
and investments to grow, and uses resources—some of which are scarce,
like water or certain minerals. Over the years, the value-chain model has
been optimized, digitized, and globalized, which has also slowed these
companies' ability to adapt to changing customer behaviors or competitive challenges. (GE is today's classic example and cautionary tale.) Ex-
tracting more value than competitors is as hard as pressing water out of
stone. As a result, most companies that sought to create competitive advantage through the value-chain model have seen their rate of growth
slow, their ability to compete become handcuffed, and their share price
languish.

In the last couple of decades, we have seen the growth and now dominance of companies that take the second approach, the platform model.[1]
Most prominent of these is the FANGA group: Facebook, Amazon,
Netflix, Google, Apple. Like the bike that is bombing down the green-
colored lane between the sidewalk and the street, these companies are,
above all, digitally driven, asset light, and quick to grow. With the exception of Apple, they began online and thrive there. They don't want to
accumulate assets if they don't need to. They don't want to own the pipeline or value chain. They freely and gleefully cross boundaries between
industries and categories. They focus on the technologies and processes
that enable online exchanges among interdependent groups of stakeholders. They feed on the data they collect from their customers and use it to
grow larger still by selling more to more.

Success for the platform company is measured in many ways: Clicks
and eyeballs. Average number of users per day or usage per user per day.
Membership utilization rate, match rate, share of organic new users to

paid new users, or customer adoption rate. Sales and royalties. Profitability per customer, capital hoards, share price.[2]

In one way, the value-chain company and the platform company are alike: They are both highly transactional. They are focused on a specific exchange, which is typically the provision of a product for money. The transactions are intended to deliver a direct benefit for the company and are largely structured and managed by the company. Apple's platform is the App Store. It has over twenty million registered developers who write apps for the five hundred million visitors to its store each week. The store generates over $100 billion in revenue for Apple and makes the Apple iPhone as useful to users as a Swiss Army knife. In one common form, platform companies orchestrate and facilitate an exchange. They match riders with drivers, buyers with sellers, travelers with hosts who have an available room. Of course, great platforms do more than just matching—they develop experiences, provide ancillary and related services, and more.

Still, both kinds of companies, value chain and platforms, seek to maximize their own value. Creating value for a customer is really just a way to make money for themselves.

This is true not only in monster platform companies like Amazon, but also in hot start-up platforms, including overnight success stories such as Bird, the dockless-scooter-sharing company. Bird began in Santa Monica in 2017 and took off spectacularly. Within eighteen months, you could use your Bird app to pick up a battery-powered scooter in over a hundred cities nationwide and around the world, from Cincinnati to Tel Aviv. Revenues exploded so fast that Mark Suster, a venture capitalist at Upfront Ventures, declared that he had "never seen revenue growth this fast, ever." By the middle of 2019, Bird was valued at $2.5 billion.[3] As cool as it may be, Bird is just another example of a platform company—susceptible to displacement by look-alike start-up competitors or being crushed by a behemoth—because it has not created a multilayered participant field. It solves only one need: how to make short trips faster.

The primary advantage of the platform is that it scales more quickly than value-chain companies and at lower costs. If Marriott wants to expand, for example, it needs to build a new hotel or add a wing to an existing hotel. If Airbnb wants to expand, it merely needs to get more listings, which cost almost nothing. And as it adds more listings, Airbnb gets the network effects. That is, the service becomes more valuable to travelers as selection expands.

Not all platform businesses, however, can generate or benefit from network effects. Platforms like Uber, for example, do not get the velocity boost from network effects that Airbnb does.[4] That's because its demand is local and additional riders don't add value for other riders. Sometimes it's the case because platforms are easy to copy. Casper is a relatively young, billion-dollar online mattress company. Competitors proliferated, such that there are now 175 mattress companies, offering virtually the same service as Casper, and consumers can scarcely tell them apart.[5] What customer is going to go viral with hot news about yet another online mattress company? To fend off competition, these platform companies try to scale fast, which can require massive investment—for example, Uber building its own fleet of vehicles—and lead to big losses. Some such companies seek to raise capital by going public, but investors aren't fooled. Blue Apron, the meal kit company, went public in 2017 at a $10 price and with great expectations. Its share price promptly dropped to under $1. There are now over 150 meal kit companies in the United States.

Another way a platform company can stay ahead of the competition is to build an ecosystem that solves a broader set of customer needs than, say, transportation. An ecosystem is a way of providing adjacent products or services by collaborating with other companies or business units and sharing data generated on the platform. Uber entered food delivery with Uber Eats, and then built out the ecosystem to include Uber Health, Uber Freight, and Jump bike and scooter sharing. Warby Parker originated as a direct-to-consumer business for the sale of stylish eyeglasses at reasonable prices, then sought to evolve toward a platform and digital ecosystem as the go-to brand for eye health, with the provision of eye exams in its stores or online.

This evolution makes good business sense. For some platform companies, it will create value. Uber benefits from Uber Eats in a number of ways. It attracts more drivers to the Uber platform, because they can make money from Uber Eats when they can't find a regular fare. It adds revenues that grow faster than the core on-demand transportation business. There are benefits for consumers too. It is much easier and more convenient to order services on a single platform than having to switch across many different ones. The risk is that there is a limit to how many platforms or digital ecosystems a consumer wants to interact with to access a particular service, such as food delivery. The answer is probably just one. This is what Barry Schwartz has taught us about the "paradox of choice."[6] Up to a certain point—which is different in different situations—choice is appealing, but beyond that point it becomes bewildering and anxiety producing.

As an advisor to companies of many descriptions, I see how the platform model has addled the brains of value-chain company management. The traditional companies have watched as Amazon climbed the Fortune 500 listing and as little nothings like Bird go crazy, and they have gotten very nervous, understandably so. Just compare the traditional retailer Target with Amazon. In 2001, Target had a market capitalization of $31 billion; Amazon stood at $4 billion. Five years later, Target was about $40 billion, while Amazon was at $15 billion. Another five years later, Target was at $33 billion, while Amazon was at $85 billion. Today, Target is at $56 billion and Amazon is at about $907 billion.[7] The scary part is that Amazon does not seem to be the exception. Apple has left Nokia and BlackBerry in the dust. Uber has become a $50 billion company, while the price for a New York City taxi medallion has plunged by more than 80 percent since Uber came on the scene. These platform companies and digital ecosystems are chewing up markets and disrupting categories that have been in place for decades.

A number of big value-chain companies—General Motors and Walmart, to give two examples—have tried to adapt. They usually make some kind of effort to go online, to achieve a "digital transformation" or build "user communities." General Motors started Maven, a car-sharing service, in 2016 but had scaled back the effort significantly by the middle of 2019. It started Book by Cadillac—a car-swap subscription service where you could get a Cadillac for a fixed fee of $1,800 a month—but closed it soon after. Walmart bought Jet.com at $3.3 billion and then folded it into its e-commerce business after it got relatively little traction. It's hard, if not impossible, for the big bus to become a bike or scooter. These companies have big investments in physical assets, such as stores and warehouses and facilities. They have long-standing, fixed relationships with suppliers, dealers, and business partners and are part of existing networks for infrastructure, logistics, technology, and payment. They have relationships with governments or other public institutions that are difficult to change or break. They have brand equity decades in the making, reputations to protect, and expectations to be filled. And they have organizational structures that are very good at protecting, defending, and perpetuating themselves.

What if there was a model that would do more than benefit only the platform owners, digital ecosystem orchestrators, or investors? What if that model didn't recklessly mow down traditional companies and everything else in its way? What if it didn't thrive on the old notions of competition and disruption, but instead benefited, indeed fostered, collaboration, engagement, and cooperation with everyone—traditional firms and startups, incumbents and challengers? What if the model sought to make everyone a participant, and everyone a beneficiary, whether they were a platform participant, an ecosystem participant, or merely part of society at large?

The interaction field model does all of the above.

As in the platform model, the interaction field company builds on a digital platform, but there is a big difference. The interaction field company is intentionally organized to generate, facilitate, and benefit from interactions rather than transactions. It is designed to facilitate communication, engagement, and information exchange among multiple people and groups—from partners, suppliers, developers, and analysts, to regulators, researchers, and even competitors—not just the company and its customers. Unlike interactions that, say, match a buyer to a seller or offer a product in exchange for money, these interactions don't always focus on just one outcome.

The individuals and groups in the interaction field are called participants because they do just that: they engage, share, contribute, comment, benefit, learn. They are not targets or partners for maximizing profits; instead, they actively contribute to value creation and can interact with each other through the interaction field.

As the number of interactions in the field grows—and the quality of the interactions is also important, as we'll see—the velocity generated produces the three effects I mentioned earlier: network effect, virality, and learning.

A key distinction of an interaction field company, in comparison to both value-chain and platform companies, is that it builds velocity to improve an entire industry or solve a larger social problem. A ride-sharing company that moves into the autonomous driving space could build velocity in an interaction field that allows it to dramatically reduce vehicle-involved injuries and fatalities. Or a health-care provider can engage its interaction field to eradicate a specific disease or condition, which it cannot do alone. In contrast, value-chain and platform companies often "give back" by donating a small portion of their profits to philanthropic organizations or social initiatives, rather than by aligning their efforts toward eliminating specific social problems.

What is particularly powerful about an interaction field company is that it can create a self-perpetuating virtuous cycle. Unlike a value-chain company that is vulnerable to market conditions and competitors' actions, an interaction field company is self-sustaining and gains velocity as its participants contribute to, improve upon, and expand its offerings and as the company attracts new participants to the field. This also means it can often avoid the kind of up-and-down cycle characteristic of value-chain companies.

The value-chain company must constantly engage in push-and-pull activities: push out their message and pull in partners and customers by signing up new members or subscribers. They pump investment into re-taining current customers and attracting new ones as market conditions shift and customer behaviors change. In an interaction field, the company does not have to target customers and attempt to lure them in. Partici-pants join voluntarily because they see the value for themselves and un-derstand that the value creation strengthens as more participants come into the field. Velocity creates a gravitational pull.

Interaction field companies are now operating, or are developing, in all kinds of businesses and industries. Not only are start-up companies adopting the approach, but traditional value-chain companies and plat-form companies have been able to successfully move toward the model—although not through the kind of half-hearted "digital transformations" or cynical "user communities" I mentioned earlier.

Rather than trying to get rid of the pipeline or making ineffective attempts at digital transformation, these old-line companies are lev-eraging their assets (rather than dumping them) to build interaction fields around them. We see it happening in heavy industries like agricultural equipment (John Deere) and industrial metals (Klöckner & Co.), and in consumer businesses such as automobiles (Tesla, Waymo), health in-surance (Discovery Health), cancer treatment (Roche's Flatiron Health), action cameras (GoPro), appliances (Haier), pet food (Mars Petcare), and fashion (Burberry, Gucci).

Maybe you're thinking that the interaction field model is just an exten-sion of social media and online e-commerce, amped up with artificial intelligence, robotics, machine learning, and some other technologies. Maybe you are thinking it is an extension of the platform model that was adopted by Uber when it started in 2009 and was then picked up by hun-dreds of other Uber-type companies—Wag and Rover.com for walking dogs, Sit or Squat and Flush for finding clean toilets, DoorDash, Grub-hub, Instacart, and Postmates for delivering food—but it is much more than that.[8] Interactions are the source of value creation for platforms and digital ecosystems.[9] But when a traditional value-chain company seeks value from interactions, it's a different and more complex story. The reason is because, when it works well, the power of mass (the assets of the traditional company, physical or intangible) can lead to extraordinary value creation when combined with the high velocity of interactions.

If you wish to create an interaction field company, you need to design and build the three elements that constitute an interaction field: a nucleus of participants, an ecosystem of partners and contributors, and a group of market makers that exert influence on the field, all of them linked through data.

The nucleus of participants is typically the company, like John Deere or GoPro, and the customers—anyone who contributes to the core interactions on a regular basis.[10] The traditional company has already established a business relationship with the participants in the nucleus, which is the foundation of the interactions.

The ecosystem of contributors is composed of partners in the company's business activity. But as part of the interaction field, data is shared between the nucleus participants and the ecosystem participants. Ecosystems in the interaction field are built on relationships that have been established over years. An example is the supplier relationship between Bosch, the automotive electronics company, and Daimler, the car manufacturer. They have a well-established supplier-buyer relationship based on the development, manufacture, and sale of electronic components for Mercedes-Benz vehicles.

The third group of participants is the market makers. These are entities that exert influence and enable the velocity in the interaction field. There are many types of entities that can be market makers, and the types differ from one interaction field to another. The US Department of Transportation, for example, regulates the automotive industry and hence is one type of market maker in an automaker's interaction field. Consumers who could potentially be attracted to the field because they want to solve their transportation needs, but have not yet purchased vehicles, are another type of market maker in an automotive interaction field. Daimler has merged the Car2Go car-sharing interaction field with that of BMW's DriveNow. Potential drivers who don't currently use the

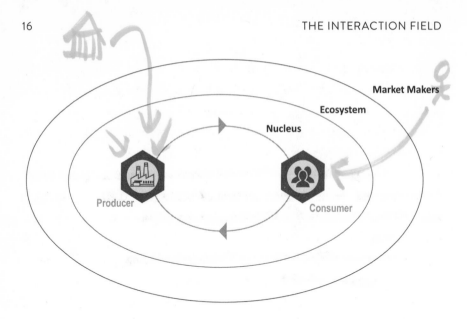

Figure 1. Three elements of the interaction field

offerings of these two companies are important market makers. The better the merged service is positioned to pull new drivers toward it, the
more velocity the field gains. Market makers can also be entities such as
research institutes, like the Fraunhofer Institute, or university researchers
that develop automotive technology.

Velocity depends greatly on the market makers. Whether they are new
consumers attracted to the field, competitors, government agencies or
regulators, or participants in other platforms, market makers can significantly determine the success or failure of the company in creating value.

High interaction velocity is achieved when the three elements of the
field work together to create network effects, learning effects, and virality.
This leads to new shared and potentially enormous value for the participants in the field, the entire industry or category, and society as a whole.
What interaction field companies can do that value-chain companies,
platforms, and digital ecosystems can't is solve a much more complex and
diverse set of needs for consumers, while also addressing the intractable
challenges of industries and categories as well as contributing to progress
on major societal issues and concerns.

← →

The interaction field model is the business model for today and for the future. This is because we are in the midst of massive global change, disruption, volatility, and uncertainty. We are seeing that industry after industry, as traditionally defined—from steel to automotive to health care—has proved to be unsustainable when configured in the conventional models. Many companies are not built for the way people think and behave, or live and work, today. They cannot take advantage of the convergence and maturing of many available technologies that enable global connectivity. They don't know how to bring disparate groups together to share and create value. They are relics of the past.

The interaction field company is the future. As you read, you'll learn about some companies that come very close to being interaction field companies, and others that have started the journey, creating interaction fields and achieving velocity. We need to stop obsessing about the platform models and quit trying to replicate the Amazon approach. Platform companies came into being in the first big technology era, the web. Kevin Kelly, founder of *Wired*, describes the past two eras and the era we are just entering now:

> The first big technology [era] was the web, which digitized information, subjecting knowledge to the power of algorithms; it came to be dominated by Google. The second great [era] was social media, running primarily on mobile phones. It digitized people and subjected human behavior and relationships to the power of the algorithm, and it is ruled by Facebook and WeChat. We are now at the dawn of the third [era], which digitizes the rest of the world. During this era, all things and places will be machine-readable, subject to the power of algorithms.[11]

The future is one of untold and unimaginable value creation and prosperity. But it is value and wealth creation with a huge difference from what we know today. It is not just about making companies more profitable or making the mega-rich into the super-mega-rich. Nor is it about reconfiguring an industry or category so it can continue to grow as before.

The future is going to be about creating value for everyone. It's about an interaction field that transcends traditional industries and boundaries, a new type of company, and a new form of governance. It's about entities that can solve the immediate challenges of people today and also the major social and economic challenges of the future.

To take advantage of this enormous and thrilling opportunity, we all have to make some shifts in our thinking and behavior.

Mind-Set. Forget the old win-lose, zero-sum, beat-the-competition point of view. Forget about disruption. The new mind-set is broader, more inclusive, more focused on problem-solving, value creation, shared wealth, and social benefit. Forget about the old ways, where companies built up assets, brought them all under one roof, leveraged them for domination, and focused on controlling and optimizing them. In the interaction field era, companies avoid owning and amassing tangible assets and instead seek to create interactions with ecosystem participants and market makers. They gather data, information, knowledge, practices, and processes, develop expertise, and cultivate values. They create products and services by accelerating interaction velocity across the field. Companies know they cannot control these interactions, nor do they want to. What they do want is to facilitate and enable them, and apply them in distinctive ways.

Operating Model. The "how" of the interaction field is neither aggressive nor defensive. It is not about attacking competitors, defending assets, preserving brands, setting up barriers to entry, or seeking protection for practices and markets. It runs on collaboration and collective engagement. Winning comes from sharing. Rather than pushing products and images out from the company onto the market, the company seeks to attract people and partners into its field through gravitational pull. Higher interaction velocity pulls in customers, competitors willing to collaborate, consumers to share data, and new participants to create shared value for everyone in the interaction field.

Company Structure. This is how the organization of the interaction field company is built. The goal is to build networks that bring in participants from well beyond the company's traditional organizational boundaries and to enable and orchestrate interactions among participants. The structure is flexible, so that it can accommodate new participants of different types with different needs. The hierarchical structure—with layers of management, units and subunits, linear career paths, and management by decision trees—will disappear. This used to be an efficient way to manage a company's resources and assets and to realize supply-side economies of scale. But, in the future, companies will organize themselves with external partners as a network—interconnected and constantly reconfiguring. In this system, the concept of agility takes on new meaning. While it typically refers to a set of practices employed to speed up organizations, in the context of interaction fields, agility becomes about creating an ever changing system of interactions among participants, adapting to changing needs, wants, and expectations.[12]

Goals. The fourth shift is in what we measure and what we strive for—how a company, industry, or society assesses value and value creation. Evaluation of an interaction field company has quantitative aspects, such as the number or frequency of participants. But the quality of the interactions and level of engagement are equally, if not more, important.

In the end, however, what matters most is how and to what extent the interaction field company improves the quality of life for its participants and society as a whole. What new and shared value is created that will make the future better?

So, as we evaluate the performance of a company that is trying to embrace the interaction field model, we should ask two fundamental questions: Does the company create value primarily for itself, or does it create shared value, prosperity, and wealth for other participants? And does it change how well companies, industries, and even countries solve the most difficult and intractable challenges of our society today and in the future?

Once you've been able to make these shifts, you'll see that what they all have in common is that they change the way you look at the concept of value.

In the value-chain model, the primary goal has long been boiled down to maximizing value for the shareholder. But shareholders in public companies do not generate knowledge or create value. Their participation is fundamentally transactional: purchasing or selling stock. They don't have a particular interest in expanding the interaction field or building velocity. In the interaction field company, shareholders and investors matter, and everyone shares in the responsibility of creating value.

Finally, the new model is holistic. At the level of a country or society, it does not merely seek to generate "economic growth"—which has traditionally been measured by gross domestic product (GDP)—but also to contribute to economic development and solve human problems at the individual or global level.

Now, let's see how the model can be deployed in a major, established industry: agriculture.

chapter two

Revolutionizing a Company and Industry

Interactions Versus Transactions

I could start the conversation about the interaction field by talking about young, exciting start-ups and how they create platforms, engage participants, and bake learning into their companies, but I won't. Even though these small, usually well-funded companies could serve as valuable examples and many of them illustrate success through velocity, they represent a special case. When you start with a blank slate and focus on disruption, as such start-ups do, it's relatively easy to create an interaction field, for the obvious reason that you don't have to change anything. They have the advantage of not having many fixed costs and capital assets. They can invest in the latest technologies to become efficient and streamlined. They are thus able to exploit revenue opportunities faster and scale more rapidly than value-chain behemoths and platform monsters, which makes them attractive to investors.

It's harder for a legacy company—especially a large enterprise and, above all, a traditional value-chain one—to create an interaction field. They have so much already in place: infrastructure, hierarchy, tradition, process, brand identity, products, networks, and culture.

But it can be done, and, when it is done successfully, the results can be amazing. It is important for legacy companies to take some decisive steps toward becoming interaction field companies. The $30 billion agricultural equipment firm John Deere has done it.

Founded in 1837, John Deere is about as traditional as a company can get. It manufactures and assembles big machines in factories, many of which are located in the United States. It has a corporate hierarchy. Its primary customers are farmers, but John Deere also services the government and military markets, construction, and home and lawn care. It sells through a big network of dealers and parts suppliers worldwide. Its machines are instantly recognizable thanks to the distinctive yellow-and-green trade dress. It has a global presence, with sales, service, and support operations in thirty countries, but its headquarters are in America's heartland—Moline, Illinois. There you can take a factory tour and watch how the workers manufacture and assemble balers and combines, tractor cabs, diesel engines, transmissions, axles, gears, and shafts. There's even a John Deere Tractor and Engine Museum and gift shop in Waterloo, Iowa, where you can buy Deere-brand apparel, games, and toys. My personal favorite is the battery-powered construction loader for kids. It looks and works pretty much like the real thing and is a nice way for farm children to get started in the family business.

Was there ever a larger, more traditional company? With its factories, pipeline, and target customers, it sounds like the definition of a value-chain company. John Deere executives talk of competing and winning, of core values so typical of traditional heartland companies—integrity, quality, commitment, and innovation—and their pledge of passion. As John Deere, the company's founder, said, "I will never put my name on a product that does not have in it the best that is in me."

Deere defines its success through traditional financial metrics: costs, sales, price realization, shipment volumes, operating profit, share price. It satisfies the quants among us with detailed reporting of impairment charges, currency translation, credit losses, and financing spreads.

But how traditional is it really?

Until a few years ago, John Deere did talk about platforms, but not in the way we think of them now. To Deere, a platform meant a portfolio of equipment intended for particular purposes or types of farms. It had its Agriculture and Turf business segment, for example, in which Deere offered tractors, harvesters, balers, mowers, forage and tillage equipment, and sprayers and seeding equipment, all to be used for crop care, harvesting, and turf maintenance. That was in 2013.

Deere is a good example of an interaction field company in the making. Of course, it will evolve and change, because an essential characteristic of these companies is that they exist in a state of constant development and aspiration.

So why do I call Deere—a traditional manufacturing, sales, and service concern—an interaction field company in the making?

Let us consider what is necessary to build an interaction field. Of course, it is a given that Deere offers a distinctive core technology or product, as every successful company of any kind does. In the case of Deere, it comes down to a ten-ton iconic green tractor. John Stone, vice president for Deere's Intelligent Solutions Group, explains that when people think of the Internet of Things (IoT), they typically picture small devices, things that can fit in one's pocket. But for John Deere, he says, "The 'T' is a ten-ton tractor." Deere's large farm equipment includes modems, Wi-Fi, and Bluetooth to facilitate two-way communication. The tractor collects data from the farm and sends it to the cloud. It also sends instructions from Deere, dealers, and software providers to the tractor. "The two-way communications tell the machine what to do," Stone says. And the machines can communicate with each other as they work the fields.[1]

There are three distinct categories of participants that grow in an interaction field. The first, the nucleus, comprises the direct users and buyers of the offering, the people that are essentially customers or consumers. They are the closest to the company and the company's products and services and typically interact with it the most. They are the richest source of data for the company and, ideally, gain the most value from their participation. For John Deere, most participants in the nucleus are farmers.

The second category is the ecosystem: the people and entities that do not directly engage with the offering, but who can indirectly participate, share, and create value. In the John Deere interaction field, an ecosystem member might be an independent seed producer. Such a company does not directly use Deere equipment to work a farm, but Deere does share data with it about farming results, which the seed producer can use to improve its products, which eventually deliver new value to the farmers in the nucleus.

The third category of participants is the market makers. These are individuals or entities—public or private—that do not directly or do not yet use the offerings but nevertheless create value. They have influence on the interaction velocity of the field. In the case of Deere, a market maker might be the US Department of Agriculture (USDA), which sets regulations, provides subsidies, and does other things that have an effect on the value that Deere can produce.

To get a closer look at the participants in the Deere interaction field, let's visit an actual field—a cornfield on a farm where the owners use John Deere equipment. Let's say the owners are a typical American farming family, the Millers. About 97 percent of farms in the United States are family owned. But these family farms are not the mom-and-pop operations one might imagine. They tend to be incorporated. Many family members, and more than one generation, are typically involved in management and production.

The Miller farm is in Illinois, where it spreads across 1,900 acres— bigger than the 1,200 acre median, but of modest size in comparison to the biggest operators. With consolidation taking place throughout the country, farm size is on the rise. Some farms are as big as thirty thousand acres.

The Millers grow corn, as do many American farmers. The United States is the largest producer of corn in the world, with almost one hundred million acres in cultivation, most of it in Illinois and Minnesota. The Millers also grow soybeans; Illinois is the top soybean-producing state in America. The Miller farm is located in the very heart of agricultural production and is growing the United States' two major crops.

Farming is a business, for sure, but it is not a high-margin one. Almost 95 percent of the 2.1 million US farms have annual revenues below $1 million and are doing OK if they achieve a 5 percent profit.[2] The bigger farms may produce $10 million to $15 million in annual sales and generate a 10 to 20 percent profit.

No farm that I know of racks up FANGA-style sales growth or massive operating margins, or sits on a huge cash hoard. Farming is a relatively small business and most farmers don't think in terms of growth. They think about survival and sustainability, of good years and not-so-good years, of reliable markets, steady improvement in farm management, and upgrades in equipment and infrastructure. And it's not getting any better—US farm income has declined by 46 percent over the last five years.

Farmers of any size, including medium-size concerns like the Miller farm and even the biggest agricultural giants, have to be smart about the management of every phase of the farming cycle: field preparation, planting, the application of soil treatments, and harvesting. That's why today even small operators and die-hard traditionalists are looking to advanced equipment technology, electronics, automation, data collection and management, artificial intelligence, and knowledge sharing to improve efficiency, maximize yield, reduce costs, and produce higher-quality crops.

Farming, then, has become a data-driven industry. Expenditure on technology applications—such as AI, machine learning, computer vision, and predictive analytics—is expected to more than quintuple, from about $518 million in 2017 to $2.6 billion in 2025.

Enter John Deere. As I said, at the heart of any interaction field company is a core technology that can be made smart and serves as the basis for a platform. For John Deere, the core technology is electronically enhanced agricultural equipment. These are expensive items—a fully loaded, brand-new, high-end harvesting combine can run upward of $600,000. Even a basic used tractor can set you back $20,000 or more.

In the good old days of farming—before electronic machine control, GPS, AI, and all the rest—a farmer relied on his knowledge and skills to set the seed in the field, determine the right dose of fertilizer, and harvest the crop. The farming machine was an essential, but essentially dumb, tool. The farmer was the brains. He operated the machine, guided it, and maintained it.

John Deere, along with other suppliers to the agricultural sector, has changed all that. We are now in the age of precision agriculture. Every aspect of farm management has been transformed, starting with planting. Today's farmer is looking to plant every seed to achieve maximum yield. That means controlling the depth of the seed in the soil so it achieves the best "emergence"—the timing of its breakthrough from the soil. It also means achieving the optimal amount of contact each seed has with the surrounding soil, so that it gets the required amount of water, nutrients, fertilizers, herbicides, and other "inputs," calculated to the number of droplets of input per seed.

This sounds complicated to achieve at the micro level, for a single seed, but the Millers plant between twenty thousand and thirty thousand seeds per acre. If they were to plant only corn, that could amount to as many as fifty million seeds, planted over almost two thousand acres. But the farmer also has to think about the macro level: planting so as to achieve the greatest possible yield from the entire acreage. To do that, he wants to set the seeds at the best distance from each other and the rows at the right width. He wants to plant as much as possible but avoid overlapping rows. He needs to conserve time. He wants to minimize the number of turns he has to make on his tractor and to complete the work of seeding in the shortest amount of time possible. He needs to take advantage of the best growing period and ensure that the plants are ready for harvesting at the right time.

All of this is made more complex because of variations in soil conditions throughout the farm. In some areas the soil is rock-hard, while in others it's soft and crumbly. It some places the soil forms into large clods that will not provide good seed contact and need to be broken up. In other spots, the soil is fine-grain. The soil may be wet in some areas and dryer in others, affecting the amount of inputs required. While some acres are relatively level, others have a grade. And add another variable: conditions change from year to year. The actions that produce a robust crop one year may not have the same results the next.

To get the best results requires precise management of the farm equipment during the seeding process, so that seeds can be inserted into the soil at exactly the right depth and distance from each other.

To do this requires data. The Millers configure their Deere equipment with a variety of add-on sensing devices that monitor and collect real-time readings about the various functions of each machine—from ground speed to material flow—as well as environmental factors, such as air temperature and soil conditions. The operator can monitor the information in the cab and make adjustments to the equipment as he works. He can control, for example, the "down-pressure" of the seed-setting gear to adjust the depth of insertion, depending on the soil conditions. To do this manually, the operator would have to stop the seeder, climb down from the cab, and adjust the equipment by hand to the required pressure and depth. Deere claims that each adjustment could take as long as twenty minutes. Using the in-cab electronic control, the farmer makes the adjustment in six seconds or so. Plus, the increments are much finer and more accurate—as small as one-tenth of an inch. Changes in down-pressure range from zero to nine hundred pounds per square inch (PSI).

This is "precision tillage," as Deere calls it, on the level of the single machine. In the perfect scenario, every single seed would be planted in exactly the right place, with the right nutrients and soil conditions and at the best possible moment. That is the goal of both the farmer and John Deere.

Now, let's look at the bigger picture of the Millers' farm management over time. They do more than gather data to control machine functions; they collect and aggregate it to manage machine fleets, plan field usage, evaluate productivity, and fine-tune processes. Using telematics (vehicle telecommunications software) offered by Deere, the information collected by the sensors in the field is transmitted to a centralized farm-management system, called FarmSight. This enables the Millers to monitor the data, and, using GPS-enabled guidance systems, control multiple machines in the field. Only the lead machine needs to be driven by a human operator. The operator provides information to the management system such that, with "supervised autonomy," another machine can track along behind and beside the leader. The system remotely controls the path of the machine, the planting of the seeds, and the application of water and pesticides.

John Deere is the pioneering company that invested in autonomous or self-driving tractors, having begun their investment in the technology nearly twenty years ago. Within a few years, the Miller family members expect they will be spending zero time in the cab—all their tractors will operate autonomously. With the help of Deere technology, they expect to be able to drastically cut the time required to harvest thirty-two acres—from one day to one hour.

Over time, precision tillage has become the more holistic "precision agriculture"—remotely managed planting, harvesting, yield mapping, soil sampling, and fleet management. Of the total of 320 million farmable acres in the United States and Canada, John Deere products work on over 100 million.

If these products and the precision tillage concept were all that Deere offered, you would have to think of it as a technology-savvy value-chain company, offering advanced products, smart technology, and data analytics, keeping up with or leading the digitalization of the farm field.

Deere is an interaction field company because it enables interactions in all three elements of the model: the nucleus, the ecosystem, and the market makers. Deere designs these interactions to solve farmers' immediate issues—such as farm productivity, yield, and profit per acre—while also solving the broader challenges of agriculture as an industry and society at large.

Connecting the Nucleus

To add greater value to its agricultural equipment, Deere has created an online presence and digital network called MyJohnDeere. Sure, it's a

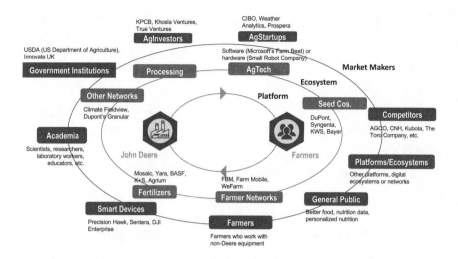

Figure 2. The John Deere interaction field

platform, but it's an interactional platform—the online nexus that enables and supports interactions between the company and its primary participants, the farmers who work their fields with Deere tractors.

The core interactions creating value are the contributions that the participants in the nucleus—the farmers—make. The most immediate way the farmers participate is by agreeing to share data they collect through sensors on equipment with the John Deere Operations Center. Just imagine the effect this has. There are thousands of farmers in Deere's nucleus, located throughout the United States and around the world. As they connect to the Deere platform, they contribute productivity data about their farms and activities. Deere then collects, aggregates, and augments the data with historical geographic data and environmental data such as the weather, analyzes the information, and makes it available to all the farmers in the nucleus. The farmer has an online window into the center, so he can review the information. He can use a variety of diagnostic and analytic tools to create agronomic reports about inputs and outputs. This enables him to fine-tune the performance of the tractors and make the farm more productive.

Now the farmer has a much broader understanding of his own industry: What the current conditions are. How others are managing. What results they're getting. Not only is the data available on Deere's platform, the company also makes it available through independent information providers such as Farmers Business Network (FBN), which, as of this writing, connects eight thousand farms and links to multiple information sources.

This is a dramatic step. Rather than jealously guarding its valuable data, Deere shares it beyond the immediate nucleus to other elements of the interaction field, such as market makers. FBN is like a massive sophisticated chat room, where the online users share information about their crops, planting patterns, and the prices they pay for goods and services, although the sources remain anonymous. With FBN, farmers can compare results by region, check on best prices, and get the kind of peer-to-peer information they would get at the local coffee shop, but in greater detail, with better analysis, and on a much larger scale.[3] FBN also offers low-cost corn seed and sells it directly to farmers. It can cut the farmer's annual cost of seed by more than half. This is particularly important since the cost of seed has been rising: US farmers spent $22 billion on seeds in 2018, an increase of 35 percent since 2010.[4]

For farmers in parts of the world without Internet access, WeFarm, which is another part of the John Deere ecosystem, provides the same kind of connection, but through a text-based peer-to-peer network. As of this writing, it has seven hundred thousand small-farmer members. They share information through text messaging and can post questions and receive crowdsourced responses from fellow farmers worldwide. These interactions take place constantly, so that farmers can share knowledge to everyone's benefit.

The value of information sharing is greatly increased as more and more farmers join in and contribute information, having more and more interactions. Simply by developing a basic technology platform and connecting its inner circle of participants, John Deere, long considered a value-chain company and operating in a traditional industry, is working toward becoming an interaction field company. This is not what you might think of when you picture John Deere. It is the nucleus of participants connecting on the John Deere open platform—as much as the technology-enhanced tractors themselves—that enables Deere to help farmers achieve their particular goals: improving yield, cutting costs, realizing profits, reducing resource consumption, and freeing up time. It creates shared business value in the nucleus.

Engaging the Ecosystem

Deere further leverages its platform to bring in participants that are not members of the nucleus. These participants do touch the nucleus and its activities, and they contribute to farm productivity in important ways to the ecosystem members.

In 2013, Deere opened up its Operations Center, an open data platform, to a number of third-party providers. These include seed and fertilizer makers such as Bayer, Syngenta, DuPont, and BASF; software developers; independent retailers; and a variety of specialists such as experts in the science of soil management and crop production, known as agronomists. (This was not a pioneering move and, in this particular aspect, Deere follows Amazon's lead. Amazon launched its e-commerce platform, Amazon Marketplace, in 2000. Today more than three hundred thousand sellers offer more than six million products on the Amazon site.)

Third-party suppliers offer seeds, fertilizers and sprays, equipment, software solutions, and knowledge to maximize yields. AgJunction, for example, is a software provider that creates guidance and auto-steering solutions specifically for agricultural equipment. Agricultural drone companies provide farmers with tools to monitor their crop conditions, identify weeds, and precisely spray herbicides on them, reducing herbicide use by 90 percent.

Farmobile is a data-exchange marketplace that connects farmers to a variety of companies, all vetted and approved by Farmobile, that are eager to purchase the farmers' data. These include seed companies, chemical providers, and insurance companies. Participating farmers install a Farmobile device in their field machines that gathers and transmits information about crops, seeds, yield, and more. Farmobile then connects the company to farmers, who can choose to license their data, which contributes to the knowledge store and also brings them a new revenue stream.

Third-party software developers—such as Granular and Ag Connections—use Deere's knowledge to develop applications that create specifications for seed density, depth, and fertilization.

Seed producers Bayer and Syngenta, as well as fertilizer developers such as BASF, DuPont, and Sinopec, have built their own ecosystem in which John Deere participates. It is called the Climate Corporation, and it is wholly owned by Bayer. It combines detailed data from farmers on yields, fertilizer use, crop rotation, rainfall, and dozens of other metrics. The Climate Corporation then sells the data back to farmers as a subscription service.[5] It also answers questions and makes recommendations to maximize yield and improve productivity. Deere also collaborates with Corteva, which offers an extensive portfolio of products, software solutions, and services for farmers—including premium seeds, crop protection, and pasture and pest management.

The value created by third-party participants in the ecosystem looks different from the value created in the nucleus: the nucleus farmers benefit directly from other farmers, while participants in the ecosystem benefit from the accumulation and aggregation of the data from all farmers. Third-party suppliers may apply the knowledge they gain from being part of the Deere interaction field to their research, development, manufacturing, and marketing efforts. And the farmers in the Deere nucleus may or may not use the seeds, software, fertilizer, or equipment these participants develop, but others in the industry, or in other industries, may. Shared-value creation depends on how the interactions between the nucleus participants and the ecosystem are designed.

Through its nucleus of farmers and its ecosystem of farmers, collaborating companies, suppliers, and partners, Deere enables a complex interaction field that achieves new levels of farm productivity and creates new shared value for all its participants. It helps Bayer and the other big agriculture companies better price their products and services and better serve farmers, all while minimizing the environmental impact of seeding, fertilizing, and spraying fields.

Reaching the Market Makers

Deere reaches out beyond the nucleus and beyond the ecosystem of connected partners and suppliers to an even wider range of participants: the market makers. Market makers can become an important part of shared-value creation, depending on how the interactions are designed among market makers, ecosystem participants, and the nucleus.

Deere connects, for example, with competitors such as New Holland and Kubota: the manufacturers, dealers, and farmers who use the competing tractors. Deere offers software, such as Microsoft's FarmBeats project, which develops solutions to collect information and manage the operation of a range of farm equipment using sensors, drones, and vision and machine-learning algorithms.[6]

Deere brings institutes and universities—such as Wageningen University in the Netherlands; the University of California, Davis; and Cornell University, all leading academic research centers for agriculture and food—into its interaction field. Technology incubators, accelerators, and investors are also Deere market makers—for example, Farm Animal Investment Risk and Return, an investor network that advocates for sustainable animal farming. Market makers also include global agencies, such as the Food and Agriculture Organization of the United Nations, and local government agencies, such as the USDA. Even the US Congress can be considered a participant in the Deere interaction field. In 2018, Congress passed a $867 billion farm bill, with strong bipartisan support, to strengthen farmers' business. (Congress has contributed to the development of other interaction field companies. Tesla, for example, received $465 million during the Obama administration to build electric cars.)

Again, the contribution made by the market makers looks different from that of the participants in the nucleus or the ecosystem. Market makers can add to shared value by facilitating network effects, but their contribution is more about influence and can be quite long-term. For example, Deere can provide data to the USDA. The agency may then use the data to inform policy or set objectives that eventually affect farmers through regulations or subsidies. The USDA has moved away from providing funding based on simple farm productivity measures, such as cereals or corn production per acre, that merely ensure growing nutritional needs are met (about nine billion people by 2050 globally, and over forty-five million low-income and homeless people in the United States who are federally subsidized to buy groceries).[7] Instead, the agency has adopted total-factor productivity measures that include the devastating and negative climate impact of agriculture, which can range from 20 to 25 percent of global annual emissions. By changing its funding policy based on better data from the field, the USDA strongly influences shared value creation across the entire interaction field.

Achieving Velocity

For an interaction field to create maximum value, it needs to build velocity—and velocity is the result of the number of interactions in the field and their quality. The number of interactions is the same as the frequency of exchanges. Without frequency, there is no shared-value creation. Equally important is the quality of the interactions. Three characteristics contribute to quality: meaning, reciprocity, and value/benefit.

Meaning is about the degree to which the interaction expresses the intent of the business, its mission or purpose, or its brand. The collection of data from a farmer is a transaction that occurs with relative frequency, not an interaction. Like the collection of customer data by a platform company such as Amazon, it can be frequent and without much meaning. But when the data is being collected by a company whose brand promise is to create shared business value and whose mission is to improve farm profitability, the interactions around data collection take on much greater meaning. The quality increases as the meaning grows deeper. Deere has a mission of "serving those close to the land." As they say, the company is for those who cultivate and harvest the land, for those who transform and enrich the land, and for those who build upon the land. In this regard, the interactions that the company enables have a good deal of meaning for farmers but also for other participants in the ecosystem. This is a company that has been involved in farming for nigh on two centuries, has a brand trusted by farmers, and is committed to goals beyond its own corporate growth and profit.

Reciprocity is about the mutuality of the exchange. Is it truly an interaction? Do all the participants actually participate? Do they take *and* give? When the farmer contributes data to Deere, does it share data of similar significance in return? (Yes, it does.) Or is the interaction more like a disguised transaction? For example, when I do a lot of transactions with a credit card company, an airline, or a bank, I accumulate points in what seems like an interaction. But when I take a look at what the points are worth, the amount seems insignificant and almost insulting. That is all the company thinks of me and my information?

The third attribute of interaction quality is **value**, in terms of the benefit to participants. An interaction might have a good deal of meaning and reciprocity but not much value. Deere, for example, might provide the farmer with a lot of information that looks interesting but is actually generic or doesn't have much relevance or applicability to the farming operation.

There is also the prospect of new value. FBN, together with Deere, enables higher price transparency for corn and soybean seeds, which lowers the overall seed costs. Interactions therefore can create negative externalities for some participants in the interaction field. If Deere offered an electric tractor with fewer mechanical parts, this would have a negative impact on the revenue that dealers could earn by providing maintenance services.

The farmer in the nucleus will always be calculating the value of the interaction. If Deere's analytics enable him to reduce costs, cut the time spent in an operation, or increase yield, it has value. We must also look at value in terms of how many participants it affects. If it benefits the community, the industry, and the society—as well as the company and the farmer—it is of higher value.

The more cohesive and tightly connected the interaction field is—that is, the higher the number and greater the quality of interactions—the more velocity it will achieve and the more the company will benefit from the three effects: virality, network effect, and learning.

The number of interactions increases through virality. As word spreads about the Deere offering, participants join at a faster rate and the number of interactions climbs. A large number of interactions is also essential to gaining the network effect. As we've seen with ride-sharing, more interactions make the offering richer and more valuable. Finally, the learning that results from the work of an interaction field is plowed back into the company and its activities. When the whole system is thriving—the number of quality interactions growing, the three effects returning benefits—a virtuous cycle is created that keeps the field healthy and sustainable.

It is when the virtuous cycle is in place that the interaction field can really expand into remarkable success. In fact, an interaction field company that achieves this exalted state of being can become so dominant that no other company can really match it in terms of business impact. It's not that the interaction field company outcompetes, shuts out, destroys, or buys its competitors. It simply creates a distinct enterprise, unique in its composition and so strong in creating shared value for its participant groups that competition is not really an issue. It's not a monopoly because it does not prevent others from competing, it does not attempt to gain exclusive market share, and it actually allows competitors into its system.

When an interaction field company achieves this kind of velocity, virtuous cycle, and growth, it can create value on a scale that has never been possible before. Because farmers can now diagnose the health of the crop at the square-inch level, enormous value is created for the farmer in terms of productivity improvement. This improvement can solve some of the major challenges for the agriculture and food industries, and even for society at large.

Deere could only do this because it can reach across industry boundaries and blur distinctions that might have gotten in the way of shared problem-solving. For example, Deere is now engaged in equipment manufacture, data collection, academic research, fertilizer and seed development, and, arguably, communications. Deere is not just an agricultural equipment supplier, nor is it solely a farming company—any more than Amazon is just a bookseller.

As Deere continues to broaden its interaction field, it could include any and all participants in the activity we might call food. Growers, processors, distributors, wholesalers, big grocers, corner shops and farm stands, restaurants, home cooks, and, indeed, anybody who eats. As it includes more and more third parties in the ecosystem and market makers, Deere's interaction field will span an even greater range of industry segments: global food production, logistics and transportation, retailing and food service, and numerous specialist fields of sciences such as agronomy, biology, and chemistry.

So what Deere has accomplished—and, more important, what it has the potential to accomplish—goes far beyond the benefit to its nucleus, its ecosystem participants, or the market makers it touches. By building an interaction field that serves all three parts, Deere has put itself in a position to solve even bigger needs and create much greater value to the larger society. It can contribute to addressing such issues as worldwide farm productivity, the reduction of resource waste, and how to meet an increase in global food demand—which is expected to double as the global population grows to about 9.6 billion people by 2050.

This is important because the agricultural sector, as it has been traditionally defined, is currently unsustainable.[8] Its use of resources is staggering. Agriculture is responsible for 70 percent of global fresh water withdrawals. Food-related emissions account for up to one-third of human-caused greenhouse gas emissions. And 77 percent of agricultural land is used for livestock production, which supplies only 17 percent of global calories. Agriculture gobbles up resources to produce food for worldwide markets, but we waste about a third of that production.

It's not even too bold to say that, through its interaction field, Deere is one of the leaders of the global food and agriculture industry's effort to eliminate world hunger forever.

What I find most admirable about Deere is that the company has transformed itself without chopping off its value-chain roots. It did not engage in a wholesale digital transformation. Deere successfully evolved and rethought itself. It leveraged its existing company assets: technology, product, manufacturing, reputation, brand, and organizational capabilities—sixty thousand people with a dazzling array of skills and depth of experience in the business, science, and art of farming—in a way that no start-up or digital pure play could.

John Deere shows how to evolve toward an interaction field company and exemplifies the role interaction velocity has across the three elements: nucleus, ecosystem, and market makers. John Deere has benefited greatly. In an industry with incredibly bad economics, where farm incomes have recently declined to a twelve-year low, the company has doubled its market capitalization in the last five years. But, as importantly, John Deere shows how the volume and quality of interactions has a significant impact on the productivity and profitability of the nucleus participants, as well as the outcomes sought by the participants in the Deere ecosystem or even society at large.

In the next chapter, I will introduce a very different way of designing an interaction field from what you have seen from John Deere. Instead of building out the nucleus and core interactions first, as John Deere did, the focus is on building on the quantity and quality of interactions between the ecosystem participants and the nucleus. This type of interaction field has the advantage that value can grow exponentially for all participants.

chapter three

New Consumers

How to Reach Them Given Rising Expectations

The interaction field model is both affected by consumer behavior and has a big influence on it. The model has gradually developed as consumer expectations have risen and habits have changed.

The result is that a new consumer profile is emerging that is essentially universal: the interactive participant. These new consumers are making a difference in the United States, throughout Europe, in South America, and, perhaps most dramatically, in China—as we'll see.

But let's start in the United States. It's important to state that the new consumer is not just code for millennial, although the new interaction field consumer does have characteristics of the millennial buyer. I should know, I have two millennials and one Gen Zer in my family. Two daughters, Sara (twenty-five) and Sophie (twenty-four), and one son, Julian (twenty). They all display the habits and attitudes of the new interaction field consumer, but Sara is perhaps the best expression of the type.

Sara graduated from Boston University in 2018, moved to the West Coast, and got a job at a major law firm. Sara would argue that she doesn't particularly care about goods and services in a twentieth-century kind of way, particularly brands and companies. She has a healthy skepticism

toward commerce and capitalism, corporate motives, marketing strategies, and promotional tricks.

But that does not mean that Sara doesn't pay close attention to the
marketplace. She does. And she expects a lot from everything she buys
and uses. She wants her purchases to be as personal as Google, as fast as
Uber, and as easy as Alexa. Her expectations rise quickly as new technologies and innovations come on the market. She is eager to take advantage
of deals and knows how to manage, and often manipulate, her various
loyalty groups and benefits programs. She is a master of online shopping
as well as a devotee of brick-and-mortar venues for certain items. She's
a fashionista and sometimes falls madly in love with specific brands. In
college, for example, she had a brand crush on Burberry.

New consumers like Sara have been characterized in many ways, by
many people, for many reasons. They are said to be self-centered, screen
obsessed, distracted, fickle, shallow, mercurial, hard to please, impatient,
argumentative, self-righteous, and addicted to social media.

In my view, these characteristics are positives not negatives, and they
describe most consumers today, not just those of the millennial generation. What looks like a short attention span is actually an incredibly
focused and informed deployment of time and energy. What appears to
be an addiction to social media is a calculated engagement with defined
groups or sources to get the job of shopping done. What looks like new
consumer distraction and disloyalty is largely a response to the enormous
range of choices in the market today. Consumers have endless alternatives, channels, price points, designs, and configurations of kindred
products and services to choose from. Because there is so much choice,
coupled with a constant stream of new entries into every category, consumers rarely feel the need to compromise and thus are willing to switch
brands swiftly when an alternative they favor, for whatever reason, arrives. To me, this is discernment, a conscientious disloyalty to brands that
fail to meet their needs.

This type of consumer has sometimes been called a *pro*sumer—a professional at the art and practice of buying, a highly skilled and confi-
dent purchaser. These new consumer attitudes and habits have affected

the entire buying population—people of all ages and backgrounds—as consumer expectations have risen rapidly and people demand the highest level of everything: better service, easier checkout, faster delivery, and less hassle. For instance, habitual Amazon Prime shoppers (like me) expect similarly speedy and competent shipping services from other vendors, whether or not such a promise is made. Since I can chat online with a customer service rep for any issues I have with my TV or Internet services, I expect the same from the maker of my washing machine, the German company Miele. But then I discover I can't chat with Miele reps online; I have to make a phone call to their service center. When I do that, I learn that I need a house visit from a service guy and the first available appointment is two weeks from now. This drives me nuts.

We expect technology to solve problems, not cause them. Sara's basic problems for which she wants solutions range from immediate and small-scale needs to high-level social aspirations. At the most basic level, she needs to feed herself, groom herself, get from one place to another, and communicate with her boyfriend and her family. These short-term problems are considered to be in service of longer-range goals: to settle down in Los Angeles, go to grad school, ultimately raise a family, and maintain her fitness and good health. These problems and goals are all considered in light of her values, beliefs, and long-term vision: that everything she buys and does should contribute to nurturing the environment and promoting social equality.

This is a hierarchy of needs that goes beyond Maslow's self-focused pyramid. To solve her problems and achieve her goals, Sara engages with a wide range of services—none of which she has particular loyalty to and all of which give her choices, help her conserve resources (including time), and enable her to participate to some degree.

For nourishment, Sara relies on the Blue Apron and Freshly meal-ingredients delivery services. Not only are they convenient, but they enable her to realize her goal of eating healthily and mindfully. She eats better and wastes less. When she doesn't have time to cook at all, she orders food from Postmates or Uber Eats, both of which deliver ready-to-eat meals from restaurants in her area.

When it comes to getting from place to place, Sara does not immediately think "car." She is pro-conservation, anti–fossil fuel, and does not like to take on debt. For shorter journeys, she gets around on foot or by bike or Bird scooter. When she's running late or has to travel more than a mile or so, she ride-shares with Uber or Lyft. She gets speed, convenience, and flexibility, and she benefits from the network effects of participation. She avoids debt, doesn't have to worry about car maintenance, and limits her contribution to traffic congestion and environmental pollution.

You see, for the new consumer, *every commercial interaction is both a personal solution and a social statement.* But I am not saying that Sara is completely satisfied with her life as a consumer. In fact, she is increasingly frustrated with the companies and platforms she engages with. That's because so many of them are not truly interaction field enterprises. They claim to be interactional. They say they value the "whole Sara." But they remain largely transactional, stuck at the platform stage. Blue Apron, Amazon, Uber—they don't really know Sara or care about her participation. They collect her data to improve their operations and tailor their offerings, but they expect more from her: they want her to rate their service, to leave reviews and personalized comments, and to know if she would recommend their offering to a friend.

Sara has largely given up doing any of those things, because doing so adds nothing to her life or experience, and none of her suggestions seem to end up as improvements to the services, and thus the whole game is meaningless. If she takes a Lyft ride from her apartment to her office, a journey of maybe two miles, and it goes OK—no big delays, no major accident, no annoying political discussion with the driver—does she have to rate it AWESOME? Five stars for the driver who just does what needs to be done? Does she have to tip the guy? Likewise, can she really believe the recommendations that pop up on Google or the reviews posted on Amazon?

That is not even to mention the transgressions of social media companies, particularly Facebook, that present themselves as forward-thinking and socially conscious, with innocent or even altruistic goals of bringing people together. Facebook should be the ultimate interaction field company. But then we discover that the company sees personal data as a commodity to be mined and leveraged to extract more cash value from each Facebook member, data that is sold to third parties—including hate groups and foreign governments—for profit.

No wonder Sara and the new consumers are often frustrated and sometimes cranky. A platform business is a powerful thing, and platform companies such as Amazon Marketplace and Uber remain fixtures of Sara's life, as they are for millions of others. She may rant and complain about them, but she doesn't stop using them. She will stop, however, as soon as something better, richer, truer, and more genuinely interactive is available.

The platform model is in danger. All those millions and billions of new consumers who seem committed to Uber and Amazon are ready to go somewhere else to take care of what matters to them: eating, shopping, getting around town. Sure, Uber makes it more convenient for me to get from point A to point B, but I am not deeply committed to the company. I have alternatives. I can still hail a yellow cab. I can ride my bike. I can take another ride-sharing service or the subway. I can rent a Zipcar. I can pick up a scooter on the sidewalk and cut through traffic. The platform model is transitional at best.

That's because there is no stopping consumer expectations. As more companies develop the interaction field model, the new consumers will expect more and be ready to genuinely engage, participate, be heard, and access solutions that more perfectly solve their problems and fit with their social vision.

So what will the new and improved mobility product look like? It won't be a solution or platform built by a single company. Instead it will be a mash-up of many different companies, platforms, and ecosystem participants. It will be an interaction field model either built from scratch or orchestrated by the interaction field company. It will be enormously capable. It will take into account the daily context of consumers, such as traffic status and weather conditions. It will be simple and holistic: rather than have twelve apps, one for each service, I will be able to get a ride of some kind with one click and one charge.

This hypothetical interaction field company will not stand still. It will engage with its consumers in a virtuous cycle, embedding itself more and more deeply into the lives of consumers. It will enable all participants in the interaction field to provide services and make money: bike-sharing firms like Citi Bike in New York, scooter services like Lime or Bird, car-sharing companies like Zipcar, ride-sharing services like Uber, any of the public transportation options, and your own car, whether you bought it outright or have a lease or subscription.

The solution needs to accurately predict the best options for consumer mobility, and for all participants offering mobility solutions, anytime and anywhere. It is no longer just about meeting or satisfying consumers' desires; the system needs to find ways to anticipate their needs, in a world where those needs are constantly evolving, and find ways to make consumers cocreators or coproducers of value. The platform model primarily serves a single need or narrow set of needs. In the future, the solution will have to continuously evolve and serve multiple new, adjacent needs.[1] That system, in other words, will be a well-developed interaction field.

We are not there yet. And we won't get there unless we empower participants. Enough of empty claims of "customer centricity" and "customer obsession"! This is the language of the self-centered company that thinks it can know, in its infinite wisdom, what the "target customer" wants and needs—not by enabling participation, but rather by asking meaningless survey questions. Such posturing erroneously assumes that customers are the only participants who affect the way products and services are developed, improved, and distributed. It overemphasizes the role of consumers in the interaction field. It assumes the consumers know and can articulate their needs and wants, both today and in the future.

Sara is pushing back against the old mind-set. So are millions of consumers everywhere.

The Opportunity

Many companies know this. That's why so many are working hard and fast to transform from the platform model to the interaction field, including Apple, Google, and Facebook, as well as two Chinese companies that may be less familiar to Western readers: Alibaba and Tencent, which we'll discuss in a moment.

These companies are running hard in the direction of the interaction field for an obvious reason: huge opportunity awaits. Worldwide, consumer spending totals some $40 trillion, and interaction field companies could eventually take a significant percentage of that amount. The United States accounts for about $3.6 trillion, and already about $450 billion, or roughly 14 percent of total retail, is generated through e-commerce. In China, total retail sales amount to about $5.6 trillion, and an astounding 21 percent comes from e-commerce.[2] Think of the possibilities.

However, many companies are actually galloping in the wrong direction. One standard approach for a traditional company seeking to create a platform is to set up a new, discrete business unit charged with building the platform business. It typically is designed to serve a specific customer need, solve a particular problem, or, more likely, to play catch-up with a competitor.

In the automotive industry, for example, established carmakers such as BMW and Mercedes-Benz saw that consumers like Sara were increasingly choosing alternatives to car ownership to solve their transportation needs. These consumers were engaging with some of the companies I have talked about already, including Zipcar, Uber, Lyft, Bird, and Lime. Carmakers came face-to-face with the reality that not everybody aspires to own a car. Many people do not necessarily care about cars and do not want to invest in one. The carmakers found that a startling number of people—including my daughter—even think that car ownership is a bad idea for them personally and for the world at large. This was a difficult realization for the traditional players, who for decades have deeply believed that car ownership is a central desire for the modern human being. So, seeking to respond to customer needs and be more customer centric, companies started to talk about mobility solutions, including subscription services, but they were still doubling down on cars.

Some carmakers tried to set up platform services. To compete with rental-car company Zipcar, BMW launched DriveNow and Mercedes set up Car2Go. They also established Uber-like ride-hailing services.

General Motors has tried all kinds of things: a subscription service called Book by Cadillac, which quickly folded, and a car-rental service called Maven. But in all their efforts, the automakers really couldn't escape the value-chain mentality and pipeline behavior. With Maven, for example, your only choices were GM models; Zipcar, on the other hand, claims to offer more than fifty different brands and models. GM shut down Maven in spring 2019. None of these services has taken off as Uber or Lyft have because they do not attract participants in the same way and thus don't achieve network effects.

In retail, Walmart has not had more success in creating a platform, even after buying their way online rather than setting up a new unit within the Walmart organization. They bought Jet.com for $3.3 billion, and though it has been relatively successful by some standards, it is still losing a lot of money and is still tiny relative to Amazon, by as much as a factor of ten. Even with $20 billion in online sales, Jet.com makes a fraction of Walmart's $500 billion total annual revenue. Walmart continues to focus on what it has always focused on: everyday low prices. To deliver on that promise, Walmart exerts its mastery over the supply chain, squeezes pennies from every transaction along the pipeline, and ruthlessly curates selection, limits choice, and pays little attention to customer interaction. These are not the characteristics most valued by interaction field participants. Yes, they care about price, but as only one factor in the calculus.

Traditional companies like Walmart and Mercedes, which build platform businesses as sidelines, can never fully commit to them. For BMW, the company's soul is still about building the ultimate driving machine. It nurtures its mobility-solution businesses in an attempt to meet those pesky customer needs and respond to new consumer attitudes. But the company's real goal remains as always: to sell more cars (some percentage perhaps powered with electricity), at higher retail prices and to more people, and to keep their current owners from defecting.

Another motivation for a traditional company to create a platform, it must be noted, is a well-known and relatively new syndrome: FOMO, or fear of missing out. Traditional companies know very well about disruption, the failure of markets, and the creation of dinosaur corporations, and they do not want to be left behind. Sometimes, in a half-hearted attempt to catch the wave, a company will simply create some kind of online presence, establish a loyalty program, or set up a membership group, flexible lease program, or subscription service. It may look like a platform, but it isn't, and it certainly isn't an interaction field. The programs are designed to lock the consumer into the brand and its products and to make it inconvenient for the consumer to leave. Such platforms don't produce meaningful interactions.

For example, I'm a runner and a member of the Nike Run Club (formerly known as Nike+). I share my performance information with Nike (over ten thousand kilometers of running), and in return I get access to "everything Nike" through a website or the Nike app, including some new content like running classes or instructional workout videos. With the app I can "find the right gear faster" (all Nike, of course), check the status of recent orders, and receive alerts about new products before nonmembers do.

But where are the interactions? Nike is a great brand, but I don't feel engaged with it. I am not a participant. I don't contribute to the creation of real value for me, for them, for others, or toward the goal of greater fitness or health. No, my Nike Run Club membership is just a nice-to-have extra service for me and perhaps a useful marketing tool for Nike. They want to be helpful in my exercise, fitness, and health activities, and they also want to sell me more stuff, so they will use all the information I give them to do so.

Again, like so many other solutions we have discussed, what appears to be interactional is actually transactional. This is particularly disappointing because Nike and many of its major competitors have other opportunities to create an interaction field. Think about it: running or any regular physical activity or training is part of every athlete's weekly routine. Even those of us who live more sedentary lives get out there at times, knowing the benefits of physical activity.

To create an interaction field, Nike would need to define itself as a company that helps people live long and healthy lives, rather than just as a manufacturer and marketer of footwear, apparel, equipment, accessories, and services. To do so, Nike would have to think of its data entirely differently. Nike data should not be seen as an additional benefit for consumers or as a way of encouraging preference for Nike products so the company can sell more stuff. Rather, data should be deployed to attract ecosystem partners and market makers who can help Nike participants understand the importance of regular exercise to their physical, mental, and social well-being. Nike could help us learn what combinations of activities—at which levels of intensity and frequency, as well as with what kind of dietary regimen—would be most beneficial to specific types of participants. This Nike interaction field could attract third-party participants who would offer products and services to provide new-to-the-world solutions for many of the illnesses, diseases, and maladies of our lives, thereby creating more health and happiness. I believe that, eventually, Nike can and will get there. So what are they waiting for?

Today's approaches to building a platform—establishing a new unit, buying a start-up, creating a half-hearted online presence or new app, or deploying data, technology, and analytics to personalize or hyper-personalize offerings—are corporate Band-Aids. They don't put the interactions—the creation of value through data—at the center of the enterprise. They are marginal at best. Ultimately, what the new business generates won't be enough to replace the drop in the existing core business. It's just a replay of the scenario we have seen so many times before.

It's a bit weird that successful platform companies have so much trouble moving to the interaction field model. After all, platform companies—including Amazon, Uber, Airbnb, and Facebook—focus on the connections with their online participants in the nucleus, and they know the tremendous value of the data their participants provide. They focus sharply on the metrics that pertain to data generation: eyeballs, clicks, converts, users. They invest heavily in technologies—AI, machine learning, and analytics—that enable them to bring in participants, achieve network effects, gather more data, and analyze it in more ways to make their platform better. They buy, rent, or acquire users. Everything they do is to create more users or usage, build the user base, and collect more data.

But these sophisticated platform companies don't genuinely understand the way interaction fields work. They still think in terms of volume and quantitative metrics. Facebook touches 2.5 billion people every day and yet still obsesses over DAU (daily active users) and MAU (monthly active users). Facebook's goal is to continue to increase the number of users so it can monetize the interactions through advertising, which is why the company often argues it is a channel, not a publisher. Facebook does not truly engage the nucleus, work to build the ecosystem, or reach out to market makers to add value. Platforms like Facebook miss out entirely on the opportunity represented by the interaction field.

Similarly, Airbnb thinks mainly about the cut it takes on rentals. Let's get as many apartments on our platform as possible. If we build out the network of additional service providers, travelers will come. *Cha-ching!* Adding Airbnb Experiences? Just another way to make an extra buck or move more units. Amazon, too, wants to bring in as many Prime customer accounts as it can, now at one hundred million people. Uber counts the number of riders in the network and number of rides taken, and offers free rides to attract new customers and convert others from competing services. These platform companies predominately care about growth—but it is virtually the same kind of growth that has been the obsession of value-chain companies for more than a century.

It is the old game. In order to achieve world domination (and, perhaps most importantly, to satisfy investors or shareholders), platform companies scale up globally as quickly as possible. They don't build the interaction field and they ignore the ecosystem and the market. It is a mad scramble to recruit new drivers, attract new riders, identify people with availability in their apartment, houseboat, castle, or yurt. It is also expensive. Uber lost $1.8 billion in 2018, an improvement from a $2.3 billion loss the year before. It lost another $8.5 billion in 2019.

These platform companies have made some rather lackluster attempts at creating an ecosystem, as Uber did by aligning with Spotify. Through this partnership, Uber users can sync their Spotify accounts when hailing an Uber, select a playlist, and have the music playing when they enter the car. That initiative was a great idea but ultimately failed. Uber Eats is more successful but small relative to the core business. For the most part, these platform players do not think or prioritize creating value for market makers at all. Uber, for example, views government agencies as enemies. Uber Eats is just a way to make the platform more attractive to drivers who can deliver food when they can't find any riders.

Interaction field companies don't just try to acquire or convert customers. Instead, they look at all participants as contributors or coproducers, and they focus on the quality of interactions that create value. In practical terms, their goal is to make the field as efficient and effective as it can be, so all participants can solve multiple challenges. By contrast, platform companies seek to make the platform itself more efficient, and value-chain companies aim to optimize the pipeline.

For an example of a well-developed interaction field company, we can look to China and the astonishing Alibaba.

The Great Alibaba

Alibaba is a company like no other: retailer, wholesaler, financial services company, and provider of media and entertainment services, logistics, and enterprise software. Founded by Jack Ma in 1999, Alibaba in less than two decades became a leading company in China in all these industries and many more. It is like combining Amazon, Facebook, eBay, PayPal, Google, and FedEx with a large number of retailers, wholesalers, and manufacturers and bringing it all together with a tightly coupled and common financial system, an advertising and media platform, an Instagram-like communications and collaboration infrastructure, and a comprehensive cloud computing technology platform that enables a large number of participants to provide software and data-driven services.

Alibaba describes itself as "an open, coordinated, prosperous e-commerce ecosystem."[3] This is the Alibaba economy, a mash-up of multiple interlocking ecosystems with a platform at the center that solves complicated challenges for consumers, the industry, and society as a whole. It is the largest commerce platform in the world—bigger than Walmart (almost twice as big) and much bigger than Amazon (more than three times as big). Look at Alibaba and you see the future of business.

Many people compare the company to Amazon, and there is indeed a parallel: market cap. Both companies show up on "world's most valuable company" lists as measured by market cap. As of this writing, Alibaba's value stands at $589 billion in early 2020.

But that's pretty much where the similarities end. Alibaba differs from Amazon in many ways: its ambitions and goals, its operating model and how it does business, the way it builds the organization and how it manages, and how it evaluates progress and results.

The companies also have very different origins. Jeff Bezos founded Amazon in 1994 as an online retail business with one product to sell, books. Ma founded Alibaba in 1999 with the goal of building an interaction field, although he did not use that term back then (or even a Chinese equivalent, as far as I know). Ma saw an opportunity to help the millions of small and medium-size enterprises scattered across China trade anything and everything with each other—essentially a business-to-business market.

Alibaba provided these retail participants with a software technology to enable platform interactions, like an online bulletin board where they could sell their wares. The technology infrastructure was highly flexible and modular. Businesses could quickly and easily set up their storefronts. Because many Chinese retailers had no experience doing business online, Alibaba deployed a direct sales force to teach managers and employees the basics.

As the number of participants grew, communities of similar businesses emerged, and they helped each other and brought in more participants, creating virality. With more participants, the number of products available increased, exceeding 150 categories and subcategories and creating a network effect.

In 2003, Alibaba launched Taobao, a consumer marketplace and website with similarities to eBay. Taobao enables consumers and small businesses to sell directly to other consumers located throughout China—not just business-to-business and not just locally, as the site did originally.

To make Taobao work, Alibaba essentially had to develop a national retail industry. Most of China's retail had been local. There were no nationwide distribution systems or logistics service providers. There was no advertising industry, nor was there an established offering of financial services or payment infrastructure. This was largely because the Chinese preferred to do business and conduct retail transactions in cash. Jack Ma set out to change all that. His ambition was nothing less than to "reconstruct China's antiquated and poorly developed retail industry."[4]

Alibaba also had to help create the Chinese version of the new consumer: adept at online commerce, impatient, adventuresome, skeptical. But trading online was unfamiliar to most Chinese consumers and merchants, so Alibaba created the Taobao forum, where they could connect directly and help each other. The forum was basically an instant-messaging app along the lines of WhatsApp. In order to enable the online transactions, and get beyond the cash-only predilection, Alibaba introduced a payment system called Alipay, now known as Ant Financial.

These infrastructure capabilities worked to shape the field and get Chinese consumers into the new mode. On Taobao, small businesses could open a "store" and list up to fifty products without paying Alibaba a fee. Consumers shopping on Taobao could make their purchases directly from the virtual stores and pay Alibaba nothing—no commission, no fee.

Taobao created enormous interaction velocity, causing products, categories, and subcategories to grow like wildflowers. Pretty soon, the consumer could buy almost anything on Taobao, from a dog translator to help you better understand and connect with Fido, to an inflatable labyrinth maze. It had some of the characteristics of a garage sale, of the high street in a Chinese village, and of eBay.

The fantastic and almost crazy variety of offerings created a windfall of social media chatter and powered the viral effect. Taobao enabled independent software vendors to work directly with merchants, which further increased the interaction velocity. This attracted logistics providers who offered essential services such as tracking and shipping.

When Alibaba Group acquired Yahoo! China, advertising and search capabilities were integrated into Taobao. This attracted more and more merchants. Taobao began to grow up. No longer was it dominated by small players who thought of it as a showcase for all kinds of wacky stuff. Serious merchants and important advertisers were willing to spend money to attract new consumers.

Although it charges the consumer nothing to use Taobao, Alibaba makes money from the merchants in two ways. First, merchants can upgrade their membership by applying for Gold Supplier status in three package levels: basic, standard, and premium. Gold Supplier retailers are not limited to the fifty-product stipulation. They can post an infinite number of products, receive product showcases, and assume priority rankings in search display results.[5] A Gold Supplier also receives a third-party verification of the business, displayed online, which enhances its reputation and builds trust.

Second, merchants can purchase advertising and marketing services through Alimama, an Alibaba service and China's equivalent to Google's AdSense, for either cost per impression or cost per time.[6]

Alibaba engages with its ecosystem participants, just as John Deere does, by essentially giving away information and opening up opportunities, rather than trying to keep data secret and shut down competitors. Chris Tung, Alibaba's chief marketing officer, told *Fast Company* that Alibaba "today is an ecosystem." According to Tung, a major challenge for Alibaba is helping potential ecosystem participants understand how the company creates value. Alibaba essentially has to explain what an interaction field is (the company doesn't use the term yet). But once people get it, it's a "no-brainer," Tung says. Why wouldn't they? They're going to have access to 550 million people and more data than from any other source.[7]

To further build out the ecosystem, Alibaba makes investments in enterprises that are not part of Alibaba's core business, but which demonstrate opportunity to "generate synergies through an equity relationship." Alibaba's deep, data-driven knowledge of the participants within its interaction field, and thus its awareness of areas for potential growth, allows for these strategic investments. In 2017, the company reported that "large minority investments" yielded more than a fourfold return.[8]

In the past three years, Alibaba has made 174 deals to incorporate disparate participants into its network, all focused on building synergies across services. In other words, Alibaba has built interaction velocity to create robust network, learning, and viral effects. These acquisitions include Weibo, a hugely popular microblogging website like Twitter, which integrates the virality of social media influencers into Alibaba's interaction field; a maps app similar to Google; and Hema, a high-end grocery store for affluent shoppers.

Hema perhaps best demonstrates the power of building velocity in the ecosystem of the Alibaba interaction field. There are 170 Hema stores that carry 3,000 products from 100 countries. The Hema stores are unlike anything you can imagine seeing in the West: part supermarket, part restaurant, and part fulfillment center. Most orders are made via mobile phone. Orders are delivered for free within thirty minutes if you live within a three-mile radius, twenty-four hours a day. Alibaba leverages the enormous amount of data it collects and its machine-learning capabilities to hyper-personalize the shopping experience in the store. Don't forget to bring your phone with you when you visit Hema, because everything you do inside requires it—from scanning QR codes to get product information at the shelf to purchasing what's in your shopping cart. Hema is so successful, it even beat Apple's staggering $5,500 of revenue per square foot to become the number-one retailer in the world. Alibaba expects Hema to grow to two thousand stores in the next three to five years.

It's important to say here that Alibaba's approach to bringing in ecosystem participants may look like Amazon's, but the philosophy is really very different. Amazon makes acquisitions (like Whole Foods) and then changes them to conform to Amazon's style. Alibaba invests in companies and lets them flourish in their own way, and Alibaba has invested in twice as many companies as Amazon has acquired.

As Alibaba has grown, it has been able to capitalize on its accumulation of data to develop scalable and modular online platforms and algorithms that simultaneously streamline and broaden its business, increasing Alibaba's appeal to participants from a wide array of industries and sectors.

To extend its online presence into physical retail, it signed up one million convenience stores. Stores are required to use Alibaba's Ling Shou Tong (LST) system, which analyzes sales and operations data and turns it into useful insights. LST helps Alibaba advise shop owners with product selection, inventory tracking, and in-store digital advertising to better serve their neighborhoods.

To extend its reach beyond China, Alibaba created Tmall, which enables big brands from outside the country to sell to Chinese consumers. eWTP is a global trading platform that connects small and medium-size enterprises around the world with Chinese consumers. And AliExpress enables Chinese firms to sell to global markets beyond China.

Alibaba's relentless focus on interaction velocity—on enabling interactions, not controlling them—has paid off enormously. More than ten million merchants and sellers participate. As many as 1.5 billion product listings exist in some 150 categories. Taobao's gross merchandise volume (GMV) exploded exponentially, from $31 billion to $154 billion over the course of a couple of years. Total GMV for Alibaba today is $768 billion, compared to $239 billion for Amazon and about $20 billion for Walmart's e-commerce business.[9] Alibaba is on track to deliver total GMV of $1 trillion at the end of the first quarter of 2020.

Taobao is accessed 7.2 times a day per active user, and consumers view an average of nineteen products during the course of a day. They also like and share their opinions and experiences, posting about twenty million reviews each day. These billions of products become part of the daily routine of Chinese consumers.[10]

The Market Makers

Alibaba is particularly adept—and almost unique—in the way it builds interaction velocity through its market makers. These are the individuals and entities that do not directly use the offerings or benefit from the exchange of data and interactions; they do not participate in the nucleus, nor are they members of the ecosystem.

However, they do have influence, directly or indirectly, on the activity of the field, and as such they are powerful contributors to velocity. In the Deere interaction field, we saw that a market maker might be the US Department of Agriculture, which sets regulations, provides subsidies, and does other things that have an effect on the value that Deere and its field can produce.

In the case of Alibaba, the market makers are the hundreds of millions of consumers who are not linked to Alibaba. To attract those consumers and create gravitational pull, Alibaba builds services in travel, health care, mobility, education, culture, and entertainment. Market makers also include independent software vendors that provide technology such as customer relationship management, logistics, search optimization, or call-center outsourcing. They include Taobao partners that provide services for storefront operations and marketing for consumers or brands. These market makers are distinct from the ecosystem partners such as Taobaoke, the network of third-party websites that make product recommendations; Alimama, the ad-technology and marketing network; and Koubei and Ele.me, two food-delivery services that deliver in 676 countries for over 3.5 million merchants in China.

Ele.me has become China's leading food-delivery service, which together with Meituan, accounts for over 90 percent of market. Its name means, essentially, "Hungry yet?" Of course you are! Ele.me is similar to Uber Eats or DoorDash in the United States, except that the drivers use scooters. The market for food delivery in China is fantastically large, over $36 billion. By one estimate, Chinese consumers placed ten billion orders for food deliveries in 2018. Alibaba has been counting on the Chinese food-delivery industry to grow transactions at a high pace. The high rates of over 60 percent annually have come down to about 50 percent and 35 percent in the last two years, which are still high growth rates. To capture as much of that business as possible, Alibaba coordinates its logistics data with Ele.me's, so the units and affiliates of the e-commerce giant can benefit from Ele.me's daily network of at least four hundred thousand delivery personnel.

The story of another member of the Alibaba network, Ant Financial, shows how powerful market makers can be in generating interaction velocity. The Bank of China's minimum loan amount of nearly $1 million restricted growth of small and medium-size businesses. So, in 2012, Ant started making microloans. With authorized access to extensive transaction records of loan applicants within Alibaba's merchant system, Ant's algorithm can now process loans as small as $50 in a matter of minutes.

With the ability to analyze every "transaction, every communication between buyer and seller . . . indeed every action taken on [Alibaba's] platform" to produce credit scores, Ant loaned more than $13.4 billion in its first seven years with a default rate of just 1 percent, well below the World Bank's reported 2016 average of 4 percent.[11] Alibaba then merged Ant with its online payment-processing system, Alipay (which generates revenue through transaction fees and escrow services), to create Ant Financial. Ant Financial is now the largest financial-technology company in the world, attracting more venture-capital investment in 2018 than all North American fintech companies combined.[12]

In its incredible expansion, Alibaba's platform now hosts a slew of data- and algorithm-driven services, as well as tremendous cloud-computing capabilities. The greatest benefit for Alibaba, and ultimately for all of its participants, is the huge amount of data it collects from, for, by, and about participants through the various channels and its ecosystem and market makers. One of the most important uses of the data is to bring new participants into the ecosystem, thereby creating a virtuous cycle of continuous new growth.

For example, Alibaba worked with Apple to identify some three million Chinese people who might be interested in the release of the iPhone 7.[13] According to marketing executive Tung, there was no other way for Apple to have gotten such data about the Chinese buying population or to have reached so many potential buyers.

In January 2019, Alibaba announced the creation of A100, "a strategic partnership program that offers companies a holistic one-stop solution to accelerate their digital transformation."[14] The A100 program resides on the Alibaba operating system, through which members can choose an "exhaustive menu of services to enhance their business operations." In something of a beta test, Alibaba developed "cross-platform partnerships" with Nestlé and Starbucks, both of which have utilized Alibaba's interaction field to forge key strategic partnerships in Chinese markets.[15]

Bringing Starbucks into the Alibaba interaction field did nothing less than transform the coffee industry in China, bringing new value not only to Alibaba customers but to all Chinese consumers. Starbucks collaborates with other market makers in the Alibaba interaction field, including delivery services like Ele.me, to make its drink and food offerings available through two thousand stores in thirty cities in China.[16]

The Social Context

All of the Alibaba initiatives can be seen as in service of a social good, contributing to Jack Ma's stated mission to "make it easy to do business anywhere." This is very important for Chinese consumers—especially for those outside of the big cities, and even for many in the secondary cities, who do not have access to the choices that big-city residents or US consumers do. (Not everywhere, of course. There are food deserts in the United States as well.) To enable Chinese consumers to do business anywhere, Alibaba promises to deliver purchases to any location in China within twenty-four hours, and anywhere in the world within three days.

Alibaba creates enormous value for consumers simply by delivering such a wide range of goods and services anywhere in China so quickly. But Alibaba is also making a huge contribution to developing the structure and operating systems for the entire Chinese economy, providing millions of retailers the knowledge and tools they need to succeed. Alibaba has tremendous potential for growth within China, where some 80 percent of businesses are still exclusively brick-and-mortar.

The success of Alibaba can be seen in its number of participants. The company says 601 million people shop with them, and 666 million people are active monthly mobile users. Amazon has about 300 million people who buy stuff on the site, with about 100 million Amazon Prime members. Not only does Alibaba engage with more people, it represents a much larger slice of the national economy. In China, retail makes up a massive 40 to 45 percent of GDP; in the United States, retail accounts for a smaller chunk, approaching 6 percent. Alibaba owns perhaps two-thirds of the Chinese retail market.

There is no company in the world quite like Alibaba. Amazon comes closest, but its focus remains on the platform and its expansion. Amazon does not have the same ambition that Alibaba does—to build the structure of the national economy.

Alibaba has its competitors, of course, the most notable of which is Tencent. The company essentially has the same mission as Alibaba—to enable the consumer to purchase anything, anywhere, anytime—but the two companies started from different places and expanded in different ways. Tencent makes more acquisitions than Alibaba: 280 of them between 2015 and 2018. The investments tend to be smaller than those made by Alibaba. Tencent brings its acquisitions over to its technology and platform so that they are weaved seamlessly into the ecosystem.

Tencent began with a messaging app, WeChat, modeled on an Israeli messaging service called ICQ. The company built out WeChat to include a mobile payment app (WeChat Pay) that people could use in conjunction with a variety of other mobile services and apps. You can use WeChat to book your doctor's appointment, file a police report, hail a taxi, do your banking, play games, and more. WeChat is like Facebook, Twitter, WhatsApp, Apple Pay, and Electronic Arts all wrapped into one.

The ambition of Tencent is as visionary as that of Alibaba—to enhance the quality of life in China by building out the economy. If Alibaba dominates e-commerce, Tencent's WeChat is like the digital operating system of the entire country—a super app, the "app of everything." The volume of interactions shows its dominance. There are over a billion monthly active users on WeChat. Sixty percent of them open the app more than ten times a day, with 21 percent opening it more than fifty times a day. Users think of WeChat as the home screen on their devices, and many don't download any other apps. Average time spent on the app? Sixty-six minutes. Seventeen percent of users spend four hours or more per day on it.[17]

What accounts for the high velocity of interactions achieved by these two Chinese giants? The answer lies in the way they build their interaction fields. Unlike Western companies, they did not start with a value-chain business and then evolve into a platform and eventually into a digital ecosystem. Instead, they started with an interaction field perspective, with the lofty ambition to make consumers' lives easier. It is that simple. Tencent started with social networking, instant messaging, and WeChat Pay as the foundation upon which to layer multiple services, doing it at a pace few companies can manage. These services are all integrated, a seamless mash-up of multiple ecosystems of interconnected companies in all areas of activity: e-commerce, communications, hospitality, travel, food service, groceries, health care, insurance, and banking. Not only is WeChat Pay the preferred online payment method, but it is used for offline purchases as well. Pony Ma, Tencent's CEO, says, "Now everywhere in China, in parking lots, farmer's markets, even at temples, and beggars on the streets, they all accept WeChat Pay with a simple scan."[18]

Both Alibaba and Tencent are interaction field companies on steroids. Their organizations evolve rapidly and they constantly add new services to draw consumers' attention and engagement. They orchestrate interactions among multiple types of participants and travel effortlessly across industry and category boundaries.

The Exponentiality

A key takeaway from Alibaba and Tencent is that interaction field companies are better able to stay ahead of ever rising consumer expectations than value-chain or platform companies are. Another is that, as they erase boundaries and reconfigure industries, interaction field companies can radically change the structure of an economy.

To meet—and leverage—the continuously rising expectations of interaction field participants, a company needs to go well beyond its industry or category and do more with the customer knowledge that deepens as interaction velocity increases, generating more and more data. The company needs to accept that digital technology shifts, and in some cases erases, industry boundaries. This affects long-held customer relationships and gives rise to new competition from anywhere.

This shifting and removing of boundaries significantly affects the nature of industries, categories, and companies, and indeed the structure of the entire economy. No longer can companies expect to operate comfortably within a well-defined category, because it will soon change.

Alibaba stays ahead because it endears itself as a friend to the small company, the medium-size company, the large company, and even the government. (It is rumored that Jack Ma is a member of the Chinese politburo.) As Ma says, "We want to help small businesses grow by solving their problems."

Alibaba creates value for everyone, some of it direct, some of it indirect. It delivers immediate benefit to Chinese consumers by allowing them to get products within twenty-four hours, in a country where the only markets were local prior to Alibaba. The company has built an e-commerce infrastructure that has modernized the entire Chinese retail industry. It has built interaction velocity and hence value for businesses and companies around the world.

What's most fascinating to me about Alibaba is how network effects can scale. In traditional businesses, value scales in a linear fashion. If you take thirty one-meter steps in a straight line, you will move forward by thirty meters. But, as Alibaba shows, companies with interaction fields can scale exponentially. Each step doubles the amount of distance you cover. If you take thirty exponentially increasing steps, you will have traveled a billion meters, or twenty-six times around the world.[19] That is the kind of mesmerizing, fantastic explosion that Alibaba has achieved.

But how do companies achieve interaction velocity? There are two major factors that will have a significant impact on how companies can create shared value at an exponential rate. As we'll see, these are framing and branding.

chapter four

Framing and Branding

The Sociology of Gravitational Pull I

We have explored two types of interaction field companies, one that evolved from the traditional value-chain model (John Deere) and one that was built from scratch (Alibaba). In these stories, we have seen the power of velocity, both in terms of the volume of interactions and their quality. We have also learned about the three main elements of the interaction field—nucleus, ecosystem, and market makers—and how each one, especially the ecosystem and market makers, drives velocity.

Now, we'll talk about the kinds of decisions you need to make to increase the velocity of an interaction field. Two of the most important of these are framing and branding, and I'll show how these decisions were made by LEGO, the Danish toy company.

First, a word about framing. Framing is about defining the purpose of the interaction field company and how it creates value for the participants in the nucleus, the ecosystem, and the market. Think of the way John Deere, the company founder, framed the business when he said, "I will never put my name on a product that does not have the best that is in me."

This is a classic framing of a value-chain company. It says nothing about the customers' needs or creating value for society. It is all about the product, the company, and the competition. Product, product, and better product. That's all that matters.

The Deere company has evolved, and today its framing is quite different. Now it's about serving customers who are "linked to the land." I like this framing a whole lot more than Mr. Deere's early version because it defines a bigger opportunity to create value in the larger interaction field. It defines the members of the nucleus—the farmers—but also suggests that there are many more types of participants in the interaction field that are linked to the land. As we have seen, these include ecosystem members, such as seed manufacturers and fertilizer companies. The "linked to the land" framing also allows Deere to embrace the market makers, such as government agencies and research organizations.

The framing of any interaction field expresses the aspirations of the company (vision), the reason a company is building an interaction field (mission), and the values that guide the company and that it wishes to propagate throughout the field. The brand amounts to a promise to all the participants in the interaction field that, if kept, creates the company's reputation and image.

Framing the Interaction Field

How does LEGO think about framing its business? Let me explain in a slightly roundabout way by returning to the streets of New York City. When the hot summer days arrive here, a familiar type of business pops up on street corners and in parks: the lemonade stand. It is staffed by kids—siblings and friends—with Mom or Dad standing by. The family dog seeks shade under the table. It is a beautiful sight. The makeshift stands are colorful and sometimes beautifully decorated. The kids offer lemonade, cookies, and other homemade treats. Walk up to the stand and you'll feel the excitement and energy of the kids as they attend to the business of serving the customer. One of the kids takes the order. Another pours the lemonade into a paper cup, hands trembling under the weight of the jug. Another watches over the cookie department. And another, usually the oldest, handles the money. Some kids are rather shy and wait for trade to come to them. Others are more promotional and wave and yell at passing motorists, bikers, and pedestrians. The business can be quite a show for a few hours at most, and then the drawings and decorations are taken down, the table and chairs folded away, the money counted and divided up, and the kids and parents go on to the next thing.

What you don't see in that scene is all the effort that went into the planning, organizing, production, and promotion before the stand sold its first cup of lemonade. The kids and their helpers—parents, siblings, sometimes grandparents—had to do the shopping, bake the chocolate chip cookies and lemon bars, and talk up the business to friends, family, and neighbors so they would stop by. The artwork must be created, the table and chairs found, the signs lettered, the money box organized. There are business decisions to be made about location, pricing, and the ideal time of day to open. Contingency plans and what-if scenarios are discussed. What if nobody stops by? What if we run out of cookies? What if it rains? The only thing everyone agrees on is that it is going to be a lot of fun.

This is the kind of activity that LEGO believes kids don't get enough of today. The company calls it "free play," the kind of play that teaches kids important life skills such as creativity, responsibility, collaboration, imagination, and communication. This particular form of free play ignites the entrepreneurial spirit and helps the kid learn how to be a boss, run a business, manage people (dare we say "employees"?) such as sisters and brothers, consult with advisors (parents), and line up partners (suppliers, neighborhood friends, and even the cops).

There is also a social component of the lemonade-stand business that LEGO believes is incredibly important. The company calls it the "play gap"—the great deficit of play activity, particularly social play with parents and friends, that exists in homes around the world. Parents are too busy for play. One survey found that four in ten parents globally say they do not spend enough time playing as a family.[1] Kids are also too busy to play. They would prefer social play but too often have to settle for solo play or online games. They live "low-play" lifestyles with nowhere near enough free, unstructured, and self-directed play.

LEGO explicitly frames its business around free play, the kind we see in the creation of lemonade stands. Playing should be more than a pastime. It should be about education and creativity, problem-solving, collaboration, and acquiring and honing skills that will make kids stronger and more successful in the world.

LEGO believes that the company has a social purpose. It can play an important role in the lives of children in terms of their development and the lives of parents in terms of their happiness. LEGO believes it can reduce the play gap, and by doing so shape the happiness and well-being of individuals, their families, and even society.

The LEGO play experience is built on the brick. The basic LEGO plastic brick, the original and still central product, is 31.8 millimeters long and 15.8 millimeters wide, has eight studs in two rows of four, was invented in 1958, and has never changed. The product portfolio has, however, proliferated dramatically. There are now more than 3,700 different types of pieces in the LEGO universe, including figures, tubes, wheels, and all kinds of accessories. LEGO estimates that more than nine hundred million building combinations are possible with just six bricks of the same color.[2]

LEGO conceives of play as an experience that is part real world, part imaginary world, and part digital. You can imagine a small kid playing with a LEGO lemonade stand, preparing the lemonade and baking cookies, decorating the stand, making a sale, and having fun with friends and family. Pictures of the stand can be posted online. The child possibly never left her room, but she has traveled fluidly and frictionlessly from one play environment (the real world) to others (the imaginary world and the digital world). LEGO calls this fluid play, which a kid can engage in anytime and anywhere she wants to. For LEGO, this type of play makes the world a better place because of the growth, learning, and happiness that it creates for children and parents.

LEGO: The Interaction Field Company

By now you must be asking, what do the lemonade stand, free play, and LEGO have to do with the interaction field model? Fair question. The answer? Framing.

Today, the company generates a huge number of interactions, of great quality, and with enormous velocity. It ranks as the most digitally engaged brand in the world.[3] On YouTube, LEGO is the second-most-watched brand, and most of the content is generated by participants.

Everyone loves LEGO. In Denmark, there are four political parties and everybody disagrees about almost everything, but there is a single, unified, and overwhelmingly positive opinion about one thing: LEGO. The company is to Denmark what Samsung is to South Korea, Alibaba is to China, and BMW and Mercedes are to Germany. In Europe, LEGO beats out Bosch and Rolex to take the number-one spot among the hundred most reputable companies.[4]

LEGO is also a big business, the world's largest toy maker, with first-half revenues in 2019 of $2.2 billion, in comparison to Hasbro at $1.7 billion and Mattel at $1.5 billion. It is also much more profitable than those two competitors combined. LEGO's management inhabits a strikingly modern headquarters in the city of Billund, Denmark. The company operates an impressive factory, with manufacturing modules and autonomous molding machines that churn out products to the tune of seventy-five billion bricks each year—even more marvelous than Willy Wonka's chocolate factory. If you could lay that many LEGO bricks end to end and suspend them in space, they would circle the earth five times.

You might think, given this perspective, that LEGO is a traditional value-chain company, with fixed assets, an efficient pipeline, a valuable brand, and a well-defined customer base. It is, but creating and selling more and more bricks is not what makes LEGO tick. It is an interaction field company with a distinct framing.

The framing of LEGO begins with the kind of activities that children don't get enough of today: the free play that builds life skills, which LEGO defines as imagination, creativity, fun, learning, caring, and quality. Free play is about education and social interaction with parents and friends. Free play is fluid, allowing kids to move from one play environment to another—the real world, the imaginary world, and the digital world. The lack of such play is a pain point that LEGO tries to solve.

From this framing follows the LEGO mission: to inspire and develop the builders of tomorrow. In this way, LEGO is more like an education company than a toy company, except that its vision is commercial: to globalize and innovate the LEGO System in Play. It's called a system because all the elements fit together, can be used in multiple ways, and never go out of date—bricks from yesterday, today, and tomorrow will fit together—so that multiple generations of consumers can play with the same bricks.

Now, let's look at the three elements of the LEGO interaction field. At the nucleus are the millions of children and adults who play with LEGO. That is a huge number of nucleus participants, playing with an even bigger number of LEGO blocks. If you divided all the bricks out there among all the inhabitants on earth, each person would get about eighty bricks. Combined, it's enough to build several million houses, ships, giraffes, towers, lemonade stands, or whatever.

The nucleus participants are LEGO fans: creators, builders, and devoted users. LEGO defines the brand essence as the joy of building and the pride of creation. That's what LEGO means to nucleus participants. They play with the bricks regularly and are actively engaged. They purchase LEGO sets.

The nucleus participants also have a lot of interactions with the company and other participants in the interaction field. These interactions can have a great deal of meaning for the participants, associated with LEGO's brand essence of the joy of building. The interactions can take place in exchanges with other fans in offline and online communities, on social media or at one of the more than five hundred LEGO conferences and fan get-togethers that take place every year all around the world.[5] The number of these events, and the number of attendees, has skyrocketed in recent years thanks to the rise of social networks. Today, there are hundreds of thousands of LEGO user groups, with a variety of different goals and purposes, including sharing information, design ideation, and cocreation. The sessions can take place in a large venue or at a local pub. They involve every form of social media. People post their individual opinions on Reddit or join others on platforms such as Meetup.[6] This creates new and shared value for participants. In short, while identity defines what LEGO stands for, interactions build or reinforce the meaning of the brand to consumers and deliver value.

The second element of the interaction field is the ecosystem. These participants have an economic incentive to create value for the LEGO fans in the nucleus. LEGO has partnered with gaming companies such as Tencent and Minecraft, and those interactions create shared value because LEGO learns from the data that such gaming companies obtain from users. LEGO has also worked with movie studios including Disney, Marvel, and Warner Bros. to create an incredibly successful string of hits: *The LEGO Movie*, *The LEGO Batman Movie*, the various *LEGO Star Wars* television series, and *The LEGO Movie 2*. These appealing entertainments introduce LEGO to kids and parents who haven't experienced them and thus attract new participants into the nucleus. LEGO defines the purpose of these partnerships as mutual value creation.

The third element of the interaction field is the market makers. These include the two billion kids under age fifteen, as well as parents and educators around the world, who have little or no engagement with LEGO. The company's ambition is to attract these potential participants toward the nucleus. It is a constant, mission-critical challenge, because kids grow up faster today and migrate quickly out of the play experience with LEGO. In order for the interaction field to maintain its velocity, it needs to motivate these potential customers to become nucleus participants. It is a difficult challenge because they are unlikely to be part of a user group and most likely have never seen content on, for example, LEGO's YouTube channel.

It is astonishing, though, how successful LEGO has been in building interaction velocity among these market makers. LEGO has achieved this primarily through social media, video content and marketing, and search engine marketing and optimization. Lars Silberbauer, the former senior global director of social media and video for the LEGO Group, believes that the company's success has to do with its focus on capabilities and competencies (conversations, engagement, monitoring, and moderation) instead of merely pushing content over social media to communicate and advertise.[7] He remarks, "When talking about [creating interactions, engagement, and connection], we always need to be humble toward the fact that the creative power of the crowd is so much greater than ours." Here, Silberbauer refers to the creative power of the market makers.

LEGO's success in creating interaction velocity across the social and digital networks proves Silberbauer right. Even though it was late to social media—it didn't have a Facebook page until 2010—LEGO now scores near the top on every social and digital network. On Instagram, the total number of followers has grown from 2.4 million in January 2018 to 4.5 million in August 2019, with the highest engagement rate in Instagram's history. Not even dating sites can match the LEGO level of engagement. On Facebook, it has over 13 million likes. On YouTube, it has nearly 8 million subscribers to its channel, with over 9.5 billion views in total and over 4 million view on a daily basis. More than twenty-one thousand videos have been uploaded. It is almost as if YouTube is LEGO's private TV channel. On Twitter, LEGO has increased its followers, from 460,000 to 610,000 from 2017 to 2019.[8] There is obviously a vast and growing body of market makers that will influence the interaction rates at the nucleus over time.

When I tried to understand what accounts for the high engagement and interaction rates, the executives I spoke with all credited the same thing: LEGO Ideas.

LEGO Ideas

LEGO Ideas started life as an offshoot of the Japanese crowdsourcing innovation platform CUUSOO, which was (and still is) popular as a channel for consumers to suggest new product ideas. In 2014, LEGO CUUSOO—which means "I wish" in Japanese—moved to a different online platform and was renamed LEGO Ideas.

Anyone can participate in LEGO Ideas in one of two ways. You can submit your own idea, or you can browse through, make comments, and vote on the ideas that have been submitted by others. This creates network effects because LEGO Ideas attracts more and more enthusiasts to submit, evaluate, and share proposals. It also generates learning effects because participants study the proposals, learn from them, and build on them. The network effects extend well beyond the nucleus, because

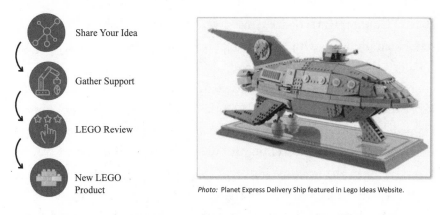

Share Your Idea

Gather Support

LEGO Review

New LEGO Product

Photo: Planet Express Delivery Ship featured in Lego Ideas Website.

Figure 3. The "Planet Express Delivery Ship," featured on LEGO Ideas
Source: Planet Express Delivery Ship featured in Lego Ideas Website, by Nicola Stocchi (project designer) and Gabriele Zannotti (graphic designer).

the participants—almost a million in number—create ideas of interest to consumers and enthusiasts in a wide variety of niches that may not have previously been engaged with LEGO. Over twenty-six thousand ideas have been posted. Interested in putting together a Saturn V moon rocket model, or *The Addams Family* mansion, or the Large Hadron Collider at CERN? Want to learn about the creators of the "SpaceX BFR Starship & Super Heavy," Matthew, Mark, and Valerie?[9] Just visit LEGO Ideas.

It's simple to submit a proposal to LEGO Ideas, but getting from idea to product is a bit more complicated. LEGO will only consider ideas that have generated at least ten thousand votes of support on the website within a year of posting. Only then will the idea be evaluated by a panel of LEGO experts. If they approve the idea and it becomes a product, the creator gets a 1 percent share of the revenue and licensing fees generated by the product.

One submission, "Women of NASA," was created by science writer and LEGO fanatic Maia Weinstock. She is a participant that any interaction field company would be delighted to have. She was an editor at Space.com before becoming deputy editor of MIT News, and since 2009 has been creating LEGO versions of estimable and noteworthy women—including scientists, jurists, and astronauts. Her first submission to LEGO Ideas was a LEGO-built courtroom with figures of Sandra

Day O'Connor, Ruth Bader Ginsburg, Sonia Sotomayor, and Elena Kagan. That didn't fly with LEGO (reportedly too political), but it did gain a lot of publicity for Weinstock and LEGO Ideas.

Weinstock tried again with a tribute to five female astronauts. The entry was posted on the LEGO Ideas site on July 21, 2016. It was almost immediately embraced by the LEGO community and got even more coverage in the media. "Everything Is Awesome for the Women of NASA Lego set" read the headline in the *Washington Post*. The website Women in the World described the coverage under the headline "Proposal for LEGO Set Featuring 'Ladies Who Rock Outer Space' Causes Stir." All the while, Weinstock kept her faithful supporters apprised of the progress in gaining the necessary ten thousand votes. She wrote, "It's been extremely exciting to see how quickly support has taken off for this little project, so to all of you who've supported the Women of NASA set, I can only say: THANK YOU. To all who spread the word on social media or by word-of-mouth, THANK YOU."[10]

On August 2, 2016, "Women of NASA" hauled in ten thousand votes and was on its way to a product review and then realization. When it debuted on Amazon, it quickly became a best seller.

What is so fantastic about the LEGO Ideas story is that it shows how LEGO has solved a fundamental problem of aspiring interaction field companies. One of the major reasons they fail is that they don't get enough interactions going. It's the classic chicken-and-egg problem. You need riders to get drivers, and you need drivers to get riders.

Many companies start with a platform like Amazon's and then build an ecosystem around it, not thinking about all the participants in the field and how to connect them. LEGO Ideas, and LEGO as a whole, makes customers into active participants who create products and attract others to do the same. They are all in the game together, so they all become promoters, which brings in more promoters like the *Washington Post*, which becomes a market maker. This creates gravitational pull that keeps the interaction velocity growing and growing.

LEGO Ideas is genius. A million LEGO enthusiasts proposing thousands of ideas for products that could answer the needs and satisfy the wants of anyone in the world. What's more, the enthusiasts promote their ideas to their followers across all social networks in order to get the ten thousand votes they need. That's a serious volume of interactions pulling the hundreds of millions of people who might not have engaged with LEGO toward the nucleus of the interaction field. Not only is there tremendous quantity, the interactions are high quality. Every post, every share, reinforces the meaning of the LEGO brand: the joy of building and the pride of creation.

LEGO is another wonderful example of a legacy company that operates in a difficult business category—in its case, the faddish, fickle toy business, where prime consumers are always growing out of the market. It was able to create an interaction field in novel and effective ways. In effect, a single nucleus participant, Maia Weinstock, was able to create gravitational pull that drew in millions of people who believe in the educational value of play, gender neutrality, fairness, empowerment of women, and the value of science and exploration. A moon shot of social good.

With its interaction field, LEGO has addressed a problem of the industry. Because children grow out of toys quickly, toy companies effectively lose participants as least as fast as they can be replaced. As customers depart, interactions burn out and velocity slows. But with its vibrant interaction field, LEGO keeps velocity growing. This has made LEGO the most profitable toy company in the world and one of the most admired companies in Europe.

Gravitational Pull: Framing

Key to the success of LEGO, and any interaction field company, is its ability to attract new people into the nucleus. As we've seen, one important group of market makers is potential new participants—people who would likely benefit from being part of the LEGO interaction field but either don't know about the brand or have gone with a different product. LEGO calls these people low-affinity consumers. The power of interaction velocity is that it can draw these market makers in by virtue of their connections with participants. This ability to attract a steady stream of new participants is essential to virality, learning, network effects, and a vibrant virtuous cycle.

Attracting participants into the nucleus of an interaction field does not happen automatically, nor does it happen through the kinds of lures and persuasions—such as advertising and promotion—still typically employed by value-chain and platform companies. Money helps, but ultimately, in today's fragmented consumer environment, without virality customer acquisition costs remain too high for most businesses to be sustainable. The attraction happens, rather, through a phenomenon I have only briefly introduced: gravitational pull. LEGO has been highly successful in creating pull through such efforts as LEGO Ideas.

Gravitational pull is created by a number of factors, and one of the most important is framing.[11] The framing, as we've discussed, defines the activities of the interaction field and the needs it serves. It's the purpose of the business, but typically does not align with a traditional industry or business category. LEGO frames its business activity as free play, a field that did not exist in this configuration before the company got started.

Any business activity can be defined, or framed, in a number of different ways, and there has been much discussion about how framing can be done. Marketers call it positioning a company or brand. An interaction field company's success can depend on how it frames its business and how participants understand that frame.[12]

There are numerous examples of framing and how it can limit or, preferably, expand a company. Elon Musk is a master of framing. He does not frame Tesla as a maker of electric cars, just as LEGO does not frame itself as a maker of plastic bricks. Rather, Musk frames Tesla's vehicle line within a higher purpose: weaning the world off fossil fuels and reducing the social stress of traffic. Musk makes the framing tangible, understandable, and real for consumers today. (Traffic, Musk says in a TED interview, is "horrible," an assessment that anyone living in Los Angeles, New York, or Boston would readily agree with.) When Tesla introduced its Model 3, the company did not focus on the car's remarkable performance, although it could have. The Model 3 is a mass-produced sedan that can accelerate faster than any sports car—zero to sixty in three seconds. Yes, that alone is quite an attraction to participants. But Tesla puts the performance in the context of the contributory role technology can play in society. When the car went on sale, long before the first one was actually produced for the market, Tesla booked $13 billion of orders in about a week.

The idea of framing is not exactly new, of course. Theodore Levitt, in his famous 1960 article for *Harvard Business Review*, "Marketing Myopia," talked about why some businesses fail to sustain themselves through poor framing. He uses the railroads as an example, writing that the railroads had not gone into decline because the demand for transport had weakened. In fact, demand had grown, and the automobile business was skyrocketing. No, the railroads faltered because they had framed their businesses poorly. "They let others take customers away from them," Levitt wrote, "because they assumed themselves to be in the railroad business rather than in the transportation business."[13]

Levitt was talking primarily about how businesses like the railroads thought of themselves inside an unchanging box, and thus limited their thinking about what actions they should or could take. In an interaction field company, framing is a matter of helping participants throughout the field understand the company's aspirations, goals, and strategic intent.

An interaction field company always frames itself within the context of the problems it seeks to solve, from the immediate and personal to the societal and global. John Deere, as we've seen, says that it is serving those linked to the land and therefore trying to solve the immediate problems associated with farming, such as productivity. Framing is not just about coming up with a different way to think and talk about an offering. Even if the railroads had framed themselves as "providers of transportation," that would likely not have been enough to make them competitive with cars, which were framed as solving the problem of personal freedom and social mobility.

Nor is framing simply a matter of seeing the product from the perspective of the participants' needs. Rather, it's about putting the purpose of the interaction field in the broader context of all participants in the nucleus and ecosystem. For John Deere, this means articulating the significance of increased farm productivity within the context of the farm crisis in the United States. Farm income declined by 8 percent in 2018, making it one of the least profitable years since the 1980s. In recent years, roughly half of farm households have had negative farm income each year.[14] Farmers must also face industry issues, such as water waste through evaporation, and larger social challenges. The potential exists to increase productivity such that it would effectively avert the food shortages that are predicted to hit, as the result of rapid population growth, in 2050.

Uber illustrates another important lesson of framing, the need for *re*framing. (Companies that compete in "superfluid" markets reframe themselves often. See Chapter 8.) Uber originally tapped into consumer challenges around local travel, the simple but unending need to get from point A to point B. In New York City, the solution used to be the yellow cab. But, over the years, the metered cab has come to be seen as a problem unto itself. The cab is not a solution anymore; it's a problem. Cabs manifest the sometimes unpleasant, unfriendly, arbitrary aspects of city life. Cab companies have not innovated since 1949, when the taxi meter was introduced.

Another solution to mobility was the black limo or chauffeured car. But these, too, produce as many problems as solutions. They, too, exist within the frame of wealth disparity. They hog space. They demand attention.

As mobility solutions evolved to include scooters and bicycles, Uber reframed itself as a mobility-services business, including peer-to-peer ride-sharing, ride-service hailing, and scooter and bicycle sharing. It then realized that it could help make drivers more productive and enlarge their revenue stream by offering delivery services. They introduced Uber Eats for food delivery, and UberRUSH for package delivery. Uber, without exactly saying so, had reframed itself as an on-demand service company.

No wonder that Uber succeeded so quickly and so well. It incessantly framed and reframed itself to meet the evolving needs of its participants. It was a way to conveniently move yourself from place to place, then a way to move other things you need around, all the while solving for the societal problem of mindful resource management. (Never mind, at least in this context, Uber's problems of management, leadership, workforce, and regulation.)

The more the interaction field is framed from a social perspective, the more effective it is in generating gravitational pull. According to Neil Smelser, professor of sociology at the University of California, Berkeley, social movements often come about in response to what he calls a "social strain." That is, interactions are more likely to be created when the frame is set so that it solves for a social problem rather than just personal ones. Lord knows we have plenty of social strains—sources of dissatisfaction, concern, and unhappiness—to contend with.

Interaction field companies understand social strain and do not try to ignore it. Traffic, and its attendant woes from stress to pollution, is an intense social strain and Tesla goes straight at it. LEGO addresses the social strain of the play gap. Burberry, as I'll discuss later, frames itself within the context of one of our most pressing social strains today: wealth disparity. Rather than call itself a luxury brand meant exclusively for high-net-worth people, Burberry has defined itself as a company offering relatively affordable fashions within a framing of British heritage and deep, sturdy roots in practical rainwear and cold-weather clothing. Hard to argue with the personal and social value of keeping warm and dry.

Dove, of skin-care product fame, responded to the social strain of beauty stereotyping. Until around 2004, Dove framed its business as personal care products, best known for its moisturizing soap. It then changed the frame for itself and its participants with its "Campaign for Real Beauty." By showing women of all body shapes and cultural descriptions, Dove connected its offerings to the immediate personal strain of dealing with stereotypes and then to the social issue of objectification and exclusion.

Sweetgreen is a casual restaurant chain that offers simple, seasonal, healthy salads and grain bowls. It frames its business in the context of "inspiring healthier communities by connecting people to real food." This is an effective frame because it taps into an important social strain: how to eat food that is both healthy and convenient. Sweetgreen connects to a network of participants along the food supply chain—including more than five hundred local farmers who meet sustainability standards—so consumers can easily find healthy food options grown and sourced locally.

Although Jack Ma frames Alibaba as an e-commerce ecosystem, he also uses a social strain framing. He says, "We want to reconstruct China's antiquated and poorly developed retail industry, and help small businesses grow by solving their problems." This framing addresses a much deeper and broader social strain. It positions Alibaba as the builder of an important part of the Chinese economy, which affects almost everyone in the world.

GoPro, as we will see in Chapter 7, has framed itself almost from the start in the context of a powerful social strain. No, not the strain felt by surfers who had been unable to capture their "sick barrel" moments. It's much bigger than that: the social strain of isolation and the need for meaningful connection and self-expression. Adventurers and extreme sports people want to share their most intense personal experiences with others. As GoPro founder Nick Woodman put it, "GoPro helps people capture and share their lives' most meaningful experiences with others."

GoPro could probably not have sustained its business if it had framed itself as an action camera company. There are too many other, larger, better-funded companies that could dominate that space. But GoPro can and has achieved velocity and a virtuous cycle as a sharing nucleus for lovers of extreme experience.

One of the challenges of framing is communicating it to the participants in the interaction field. They have to understand and buy into the framing so they can play their necessary role in value creation. Without that understanding and buy-in, there will be no chance of creating velocity.

The framing begins with brand. What does it stand for? What does it aspire to create in the minds of consumers? The Disney brand is equated with entertainment, fun, and magic for families. The LEGO brand is about the joy of building and the pride of creation. Brands are associated with certain values, beliefs, emotions, and characteristics. Harley-Davidson has a distinctive visual look. Apple is perceived as cool.

A brand is also about the interactions the company seeks to facilitate in its field. LEGO Ideas, for example, motivates kids and adults to imagine and create their own LEGO products, and it encourages them to share the ideas with others and to promote them through their social networks. It is the sum of all interactions that brings the framing of the interaction field company to life and defines the brand's promise and value proposition.

Gravitational Pull: Connectivity with Others

The second element that builds gravitational pull, after framing, is the set of people that are attracted to become participants and the connections they have and are prepared to make with one another.

The conventional value-chain company will identify potential target customers in a variety of ways. They typically focus on demographics such as age, gender, and financial status, or psychographics and lifestyle characteristics. Platform companies such as Amazon use algorithms to identify customers based on buying behavior.

These approaches may work to increase transactions between the company and its customers, but they do not contribute to interactions among participants. Only when participants feel that they share values and goals with others in the interaction field—the nucleus, ecosystem, and market makers—will they communicate with others who might want to join. This is the basis of virality: direct communication from participant to potential participant. It is far more powerful than advertising or promotion and costs virtually nothing.

Framing comes into play in this aspect of gravitational pull by attracting people who can and want to add value to the interaction field. The participants who are interested in performance cars, for example, will likely be different from those who are interested in reducing energy usage and want to see technology used for positive social purposes. Fast-car lovers may well be attracted to join an interaction field of a performance carmaker, and the virality they create will bring in more performance enthusiasts. The value those participants create will likely lead to improvements in engines and fuels, but not necessarily in energy conservation or climate change mitigation. The beauty of Tesla, however, is that it brings two framings together.

Not only does effective framing attract people who can add value to the field, it also largely (if not completely) discourages people who have different values and social aspirations from participating. A nucleus with a large population of trolls and lurkers—or simply people with contributions that do not add value—will not achieve optimal velocity. Potential contributors will be put off or drift away.

How do interaction field companies think about the people who could add the greatest value to the field, especially the nucleus? First is **motivation**. The most valuable members of the field are those who *want* to share knowledge and distribute information, to engage and interact. Clay Shirky, author of *Here Comes Everybody*, has researched the concept of motivation. He argues that participation is a matter of "cognitive surplus"—that is, time available to engage in thinking beyond the tasks of everyday life. Technology makes it easier for a person to leverage their motivation, because they can instantly use their cognitive surplus in productive, value-adding ways.

In the pre-Internet days, many people used up at least some of their cognitive surplus in watching television. Old-style TV watching was transactional. The broadcaster aired a show. The consumer watched it. There may have been talk about a show among the watchers on the living-room couch or around the office water cooler the next morning, but little or no contributory value was created there.

The Internet, however, provides opportunities for people to repurpose their cognitive surplus to become contributors and creators, rather than passive transactors. Further, social media allows for the aggregation of the free time of many, many people, allowing us to think of free time as a social asset that can be harnessed for value creation. (And, yes, sometimes for value depletion.)

There are many reasons people are motivated to repurpose their free time for group value creation. One is a desire to be recognized as a knowledgeable resource. Another is the desire to belong and to make a contribution to a group that has meaning for you.

There is even a biological explanation. One scientist found that a brief social media exchange—even with a stranger—lowers the stress hormones cortisol and ACTH, and thus increases one's willingness to interact.[15] Interaction fields, then, create gravitational pull through a framing that attracts people who can add value to the field.

Second is the **ties** between and among the participants. They determine the interaction velocity. Mark Granovetter, professor of sociology at Stanford, has written about the difference between strong ties and weak ties among people and how they affect virality and network effects. Strong ties, says Granovetter, are between close friends and family members and perhaps work colleagues. Weak ties are ones that connect acquaintances and others we may not feel personally close to but have some association with.

Granovetter's most powerful assertion is that connections through strong ties are not the best way to introduce and spread new ideas. Why? Because those people already know each other. Even if your message is sticky and popular, if it spreads only through strong ties, it will just keep bouncing around the community of people who already know about it. That's why weak ties are most important to making something go viral. If I pass along an idea about a product or service to someone I don't have a strong tie with and that person is interested, she may pass it along to her network, which contains people I don't know and wouldn't reach otherwise. Soon, the idea is exploding from network to network, rather than circulating around and around in a closed loop.

Gravitational pull is also heightened thanks to a phenomenon described as the "three degrees of influence," proposed by Nicholas A. Christakis and James H. Fowler in 2007. The two found that social networks have, not too surprisingly, great influence on people's behavior. What was, and remains, surprising is that social influence does not end with the people to whom a person has strong or direct ties. We influence our friends and family members, who in turn influence their friends. Our ideas, actions, and opinions, then, influence people we have never met and to whom we have only weak or indirect ties.

The influence does not go on forever, however. Christakis and Fowler posit that diverse phenomena "ripple through our network, having an impact on our friends (one degree), our friends' friends (two degrees), and even our friends' friends' friends (three degrees). Our influence gradually dissipates and ceases to have a noticeable effect on people beyond the social frontier that lies at three degrees of separation."[16]

Interaction field companies cannot build the nucleus just by reaching direct connections. That is why it is so important to bring indirect participants into the ecosystem and market makers—because all of these people bring in new realms of connections beyond the scope of the interaction field nucleus.

Another factor in gravitational pull is **collective intelligence**: how shared intelligence emerges from the collaboration, collective efforts, and competition of many individuals. As Dirk Helbing of the Swiss Federal Institute of Technology in Zurich puts it, "Each individual is considered excitable (by others!) depending on the proximity and density of neighbors, as well as the direction of influence." The key mechanism of influence: interaction.[17]

Patagonia provides a good illustration of how gravitational pull grows with strength at the core—that is, the nucleus of direct buyers, participants, producers, and users. Patagonia frames its activity as a mission to celebrate and preserve the natural environment. To create strong gravitational pull, Patagonia introduced the "Worn Wear" initiative. The program enables and encourages people to "repair, share and recycle" their Patagonia gear. The company states that they believe "one of the most responsible things we can do as a company is make high-quality stuff that lasts for years, so you don't have to buy more of it." By keeping one's Patagonia gear in use for nine months beyond normal, the participant can, according to Patagonia, "reduce the related carbon, water and waste footprints by 20–30%."[18]

The "Worn Wear" initiative pulls in multiple participants, starting with passionate Patagonia user-advocates (of which there are many). Their shared belief system creates gravitational pull in the nucleus. Then it draws people, like me, who do not buy or use Patagonia stuff. It attracts people who simply believe in this kind of corporate responsibility and want to promote it. They connect with each other and with the company.

In this way, the initiative helps Patagonia extend its interaction field to other participants.

Participants in an interaction field feel as if they are part of a community, rather than consumers transacting with a pipeline company. Christakis and Fowler talk about network communities, which are defined as groups of people who are much more connected to one another than they are to other groups of connected people in other parts of the network.[19]

But these communities can be difficult to create in industries where there are built-in frictions and inefficiencies. In the next chapter, we'll see how those obstacles can be removed or improved and how the resulting increase in the interaction velocity has an impact on not only the company but the entire industry.

chapter five

Innovation

How a Traditional Company Can Act Like a Start-Up

Gisbert Rühl is not necessarily the kind of CEO you would expect to find as the head of an interaction field company. You certainly wouldn't put his firm, Klöckner & Co., in the same league as platform leaders like Apple and Facebook. But Rühl and Klöckner have done something pretty remarkable and definitely worth taking note of: they have transformed a very traditional business operation first into a digital platform and then into a full-fledged interaction field enterprise with admirable velocity. And, in doing so, they have changed the dynamics of one of the most traditional industries: steel.

Rühl would no doubt argue that Klöckner had little choice but to make such a move. In comments at the B2B Online conference, he declared that the steel industry was inexorably headed toward digitization, "even if we don't like it," simply because the old ways of buying steel are hopelessly archaic. Purchasing online, he explained, is inarguably the "most convenient way for customers to buy." Indeed, the kind of online marketplace that Klöckner has created will be nothing less than the "steel supply network of tomorrow."

But I'm getting ahead of the story.

First, it is necessary to understand a bit about Gisbert Rühl, because I believe it took a particular set of skills to pull this off, and we also need to explain a bit about the steel industry, to understand how badly in need of transformation it was.

Rühl joined Klöckner in 2005 as chief financial officer and was appointed CEO in 2009. (He continued to hold the CFO position until 2012.) When he came to Klöckner at age fifty-two, he had already progressed through a number of varied and relevant career engagements. He studied industrial engineering at the University of Hamburg and, after earning his degree, joined Roland Berger in 1987 as a management consultant. The consultancy prides itself on its independence, entrepreneurial spirit, and ability to "constructively challenge standard patterns of thought and provide clients with new solutions to manage disruption and transformation."

Anyway, Rühl moved on from Roland Berger to take management positions in a string of firms, starting with a developer of software for online engineering environments (Lion Gesellschaft für Systementwicklung mbH), then a financial services firm (Matuschka Capital), a trader of industrial products (Coutinho Caro & Co), and, before joining Klöckner, a supplier of carbon products and chemicals (RÜTGERS). So Rühl came to Klöckner with an intriguing blend of skills and perspectives—experience in strategy, software, finance, and industrial products—all of which positioned him well for rethinking the steel services business.[1]

As I said, it was badly in need of rethinking. The steel industry is one of the most traditional value-chain businesses in the world. The global market for steel is around $1 trillion and, like the auto industry, steel is considered—rightly or wrongly—a bellwether business. Its health reflects the health of the global economy. And the industry has not been feeling well for many years, due primarily to the rise of Chinese production as a source of steel oversupply and thus price pressure all around. Today, Chinese producers account for almost half the world's crude steel output.[2] The supply and value chain of the steel industry is inefficient and lacks transparency.

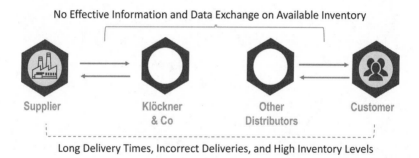

Figure 4. Inventory management in the steel industry
Source: Adapted from Klöckner & Co. SE Digital Strategy, "Leading the Digital Transformation of Metal Distribution," Spring 2019.

Klöckner plays a specialized role in the industry. Klöckner and other companies like it sit between the big suppliers of crude steel, such as ThyssenKrupp and Tata Group, and the customers, such as construction companies, automakers, and phone and appliance manufacturers. Klöckner and its compatriots are known as steel services companies or steel distributors. They are value-adding middlemen in the supply chain. They buy raw steel and other metals from suppliers and convert it into a wide range of finished products, such as sheets, plates, bars, pipes, and tubes—in steel, stainless steel, and aluminum—then further customize these products to the specifications of their customers. They cut the sheets to size, form beams to spec, mill the bars, and apply paint.

The steel services industry is incredibly fragmented, with more than four thousand companies operating throughout the European Union and North America.[3] Customers generally have no loyalty to any single services company, for many reasons, and so are constantly shopping around for the best deals. This is because steel is essentially a commodity, and there is no appreciable difference in the quality of the products offered by Services Company A in comparison to Services Companies B through Z. For many customers, steel makes up a big part of their costs, so even slight variations in price can make a significant difference. Services companies, therefore, compete on price, service, and availability.

Klöckner is one of the largest steel services companies in the EU, with about 6 billion euros in sales in 2017. The company employs around

8,500 people and operates at 170 sites. Headquarters are in the ancient city of Duisburg, Germany, a key industrial center known for its steel, iron, and chemical works. The city is also noted for its inland port—the largest in the world—where the Ruhr and Rhine rivers converge. The city is home to a number of other businesses, as well as the University of Duisburg-Essen. Despite all this activity, the area is seen as something of a rust belt. Many of the facilities, such as iron blast furnaces, have been abandoned, destroyed, or repurposed during a long decline in metals production—largely caused by competition from Chinese and Indian producers. ThyssenKrupp, one of the world's largest steel producers, also located in Duisburg, has significantly reduced its workforce in the city.

When Gisbert Rühl joined Klöckner in 2005, the steel services industry was not only fragmented but also secretive, highly inefficient in its processes, and slow to modernize. Rühl admits that when he began work on the transformation, the biggest technological innovation at Klöckner in the previous few years had been the use of email. But even that most basic modern tool had been slow to find favor. Indeed, as I was conducting research for this book, I visited Klöckner offices where I saw sales staffers managing orders by phone and fax. Hard to believe that the steel supply for massive buildings and new-model cars was being purchased via the twentieth-century beeping, whirring, and slicing of fax machines.

There were clear and understandable reasons for this kind of antiquated business behavior. The demand for steel products and services is highly unpredictable and volatile. Construction customers, for example, do not know exactly when they will need beams and girders and do not want to store materials on-site. So they place orders as close to the time of need as possible and generally expect delivery within twenty-four to forty-eight hours. In order to be able to respond to such demand, services companies like Klöckner build up their inventories so they have plenty of stock on hand—availability is key. Customers will shop around for the best price, but they are also short on time, and time pressure can trump price advantage. Perhaps most significantly, steel services suppliers had gotten very good at setting prices in ways that made comparison difficult—by using different naming, for example, or different measurements. So there was a great deal of haggling and dealmaking, which gobbled up a lot of employee time, complicated record keeping, and meant that much of the business knowledge was stored in the heads of the sales force.

The industry had stuck with its practices because, weirdly enough, the volatility of steel prices could also work in favor of the services supplier who had a lot of inventory, especially when prices went up. As Rühl put it, "The more inventory you had, the more inefficient you were, the better your results were."[4] In other words, if you buy a large quantity of inventory at a low wholesale price and hold it until retail prices go up, you can then sell it to a retail customer at a greater profit than if you had sold it soon after initial purchase. Profitability, then, was all about generating volume and capturing price margins. Knowing this, services companies would speculate, buying steel from the big suppliers at what seemed to be opportune moments. In this way, Klöckner was like a commodities trader, buying and selling, always trying to predict and respond to volatility.

But even as the supply chain was operating in old-fashioned ways, the steel industry was changing fast. Not only was China taking the lead as the biggest crude steel producer on earth, but the big online retailers were gradually edging into the market. Amazon Business and Alibaba, the company we talked about in Chapter 3, had begun to offer a variety of smaller steel products such as sheets, beams, and rolls. They were bringing transparency and efficiency to the old ways of buying, and customers were taking notice.

Other factors came into play as well. Global supply was up, but demand was in decline. Hiring had gotten more difficult. It was becoming harder to find and retain workers skilled in the steel customizing processes, making it more difficult for Klöckner to meet customers' delivery requirements. And customers' expectations were on the rise, largely because of their online experiences. They began to think there might be a better way to purchase steel products.

It was not difficult to see that Klöckner and the steel services industry had to change or become obsolete, but it would be difficult to bring such a messy, anachronistic, inefficient, old-boy industry into the twenty-first century. Rühl, however, was determined to do so.

In 2014, Klöckner developed a vision of a new way forward, which would be driven by two initiatives. The first was to digitize the Klöckner metals business by creating an online shop, streamlining the order process, and introducing transparency into pricing and availability. The second initiative would be to create an online marketplace that would connect all participants in the steel industry.

The first step, digitization, built a proprietary service platform that would, in effect, bring the members of the Klöckner ecosystem—suppliers and customers—together. Rühl knew that it would be impossible to pursue this work at the company's headquarters in Duisburg. The practices there were too deeply ingrained, the people too accustomed to the traditional ways. There was no entrepreneurial culture, especially in the corporate offices.

He might have purchased a start-up company to create a platform or farmed the work out to a partner, but he chose to form an internal team instead. Rühl set up a separate office in Berlin, a city well known for its start-up culture—populated by entrepreneurs, venture capitalists, and technologists—six hundred kilometers to the east of Duisburg. The staff of the new operation, known as the innovation unit, quickly grew to eighty people, only five of whom came from within the ranks of Klöckner employees. Not only were they outsiders to the company, they were a diverse group, representing many countries.

He directed the team to develop the platform alongside the company's IT group. This had the advantage of giving the group access to the company's existing IT infrastructure. The group decided to go with standard, off-the-shelf software, which meant they did not have to spend years developing and coding a whole new application. Indeed, within three months, they had the first tool available and quickly built out an extensive information exchange.

The group rather swiftly developed the service platform called Kloeckner Connect. This enabled Klöckner to leverage its tremendous corporate assets: its huge customer network—more than two hundred thousand around the world—its deep industry knowledge, and its trusted brand name. Kloeckner Connect offers customers a number of services and tools. Using the Part Manager tool, customers can make orders from any device, check on past orders, see what's available in stock, and look through the entire Klöckner catalog. A tool called Kloeckner Direct streamlines the purchasing process for custom orders by enabling customers to do online research into materials and specs and communicate with sales and service staff. Kloeckner Connect also offers electronic document interchange capability, so that customers can share information with Klöckner about their businesses and product usage. Additionally, customers can work with Klöckner to automate some of their processes, such as inventory tracking, writing purchase orders, and recording and paying invoices.

Kloeckner Connect had a huge and almost immediate effect on the way the company did business with its customers. Because Klöckner could interact more quickly and transparently with customers, learning their needs and goals, the company was able to reduce the amount of product inventory, which had been increasing costs and reducing margins.

Over time, Klöckner created additional digital tools and integrated them into the organization. It launched an online shop—including a contract portal and order transparency tool—solely for its German customers, then made it available in other countries as well. Later, it launched the Klöckner Marketplace, which includes over thirty third-party vendors offering complementary products. Eventually, the company organized all its digital initiatives under Kloeckner.i. By 2022, Klöckner expects 60 percent of the group's sales to be generated via digital channels, which will lead to significant improvements in the efficiencies of all Klöckner operations and also an increase in sales of higher-value-added products and services. Needless to say, all of this was very new for people in an industry where email was a novelty and fax was still an accepted way to place orders.

What is particularly interesting about the development of Kloeckner.i was the way Rühl made sure that the new innovation unit, and its online offerings, did not supplant the corporate staff. This was one reason for choosing Berlin as the location. "If the digital hub is too far away from the corporate hub, it will have no impact" on how corporate operates, Rühl said. But if it is too close, the corporate culture will overwhelm strategy and the innovation unit will "lose its start-up approach."

It was not only a matter of physical proximity, but of processes, behaviors, and culture. Rühl saw that it would be necessary to "bring digitalization" to corporate, or it would never completely take hold throughout the company's multiple locations worldwide. To bring corporate along, Klöckner did not attempt to immediately and completely transform its managers and staffers into digital entrepreneurs, but rather to bring the best of both cultures together. As Rühl puts it, the intent was "to achieve competitive advantages through the combination of domain expertise and platform expertise."

So the Kloeckner Connect platform is an interesting blend of the old and the new. In order to set up an account or get login information, a customer must connect with a Klöckner sales rep or local branch office. That means that old relationships can be preserved and enriched. Similarly, if a customer wants to make changes to an order placed online, or if there are problems with an order, they are instructed to be in touch with their account manager.

Just as the Klöckner sales and service staff was accustomed to autonomy and secrecy, the corporate managerial culture was not inclined toward risk-taking, change, and the potential failure that went along with digital transformation. "Success at Klöckner was the absence of failure," Rühl said. That's how you climbed the corporate ladder, by not making mistakes and not presiding over projects that failed.

So Rühl established a protocol of nonhierarchical communication. That meant, essentially, that anybody in the company could communicate with anybody else, regardless of where they fell on the org chart. Rühl and senior leaders found themselves in conversation with people within the company whom they did not know or did not ordinary deal with. This increased the amount of learning that was going on and reduced the corporate tendency to affix blame when something wasn't quite right. What had been transactional became interactional.

To further supplement learning, Klöckner instituted a policy that allowed employees to take online courses on company time. In collaboration with the University of Duisburg-Essen, the Berlin School of Digital Business, and the Haufe Group, which offers consulting and training services, Klöckner made it possible and relatively painless for employees to learn about the digital world of today and tomorrow.

Another program is known as the Digital Experience Program, which enables exchanges, learning, and information transfer between Kloeckner.i and sales employees from different branches of the company. Sales employees take on assignments of a month or two to learn about digitization processes.

My favorite innovation is what Rühl calls, in public, "failure nights," although they are known internally as "fuck-up nights." These are evening get-togethers in which employees and entrepreneurs talk about their failures and what they learned from them. They are extremely popular events and have gone a long way to changing the corporate view of failure. Employees now see it as a source of information and knowledge that can be applied to new initiatives and improve the business.

The next step asked even more of Klöckner people. The company moved to expand the platform beyond the customer-supplier ecosystem to the wider market, including competitive and complementary suppliers. The idea was to create a marketplace, rather like the ones on Amazon Business and Alibaba, that would essentially bring the entire industry onto one platform and facilitate interactions among all participants.

The result, launched in early 2017, is XOM Materials (pronounced "zhawm"). It's an open industry platform, an online marketplace, an interaction field. It opens the market up to other vendors, offering a wide range of standard products, custom products, and complementary products, from Klöckner and from a number of competitive suppliers and services providers. Customers can do online in a matter of moments what had taken endless phone calls and faxes before. With a single email, they can initiate a check on availability and price guidance from multiple vendors for a given order.[5]

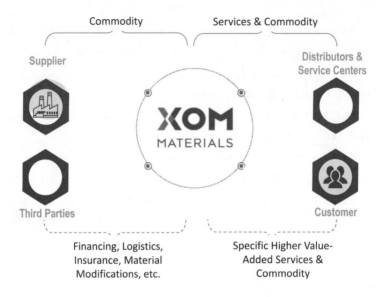

Figure 5. XOM Materials open industry platform
Source: Adapted from Klöckner & Co. SE Digital Strategy, "Leading the Digital Transformation of Metal Distribution," Summer 2018.

In order to bring in competitors—who have always jealously guarded their customers, data, and pricing—Klöckner created XOM as a separate entity, independent of the company. While Klöckner owns 50 percent of the venture, it has no special rights or any more access to data or functionality than any other participant. XOM operates from its own office, run by its own management team, and with independent financial management.

In addition to products from a variety of vendors, customers can engage with suppliers of complementary products and services—the market makers—including financing companies, logistics managers, and shipping. Customers can achieve efficiencies as never before, such as combining orders from two suppliers in a single shipment.

XOM has achieved remarkable velocity, opening new offices in Atlanta and other locations. It has grabbed, and will continue to grab, market share, due to the high frequency of transactions—the network effect. As XOM catches on, virality kicks in. Additional suppliers, and suppliers of other kinds of materials and services, will want to join. If XOM works for metal pipes, it can work for plastic pipes too.[6]

Within two years, the Klöckner ecosystem was generating a billion dollars in sales. Today, Klöckner is at the center of an industry-wide interaction field that has transformed the steel distribution business. It brings together customers around the world and connects them with one another, with suppliers and partners, and with competitors. It provides participants with the kind of data and information they hunger for. The company now describes itself as "one of the leading steel service center companies worldwide" and "a pioneer of the digital transformation in the steel industry."

But XOM is not alone in the effort to transform the steel industry. Zhaogang is a big Chinese platform that supports 10 percent of the trade in the domestic market, a sales volume equivalent to 60 percent of the US market. ThyssenKrupp operates Materials4Me, serving ninety thousand customers per year. Alibaba also continues to build out its business-to-business platform.

The Klöckner story is largely about how to reduce inefficiencies and frictions in an entire industry. They did it with their own platform, Kloeckner.i, and the industry marketplace XOM. Reducing inefficiencies freed up resources, which Klöckner used to expand into higher-value-added products and services. Creating transparency eliminated the need for price arbitrage.

The data generated in the Klöckner interaction field is of great value. Access to such extensive data will completely change the planning process, which has long been short-sighted and relatively ad hoc. Now, with much more data available and accessible, companies will be able to get much smarter about stocking, delivery, and sales tracking.

This will only get better as the learning effects kick in. Machine learning will allow companies to do more with their data, including optimizing material sourcing, making process adjustments more efficient, and enabling cost-effective advanced metal production capabilities. Virtual reality will allow companies to streamline remote steel plant operations. Blockchain will provide faster and more reliable ways to authenticate materials. Increased implementation of cloud-based technologies will facilitate the integration of supply-chain processes and tools. More supply-chain visibility and root-cause analyses will help companies fulfill specific business performance goals.

An important success factor has been how Klöckner enabled its customers to connect with the platform. It was careful to include corporate and sales staff in its transformation. The design of the platform respected the existing relationships among sales reps, local branch offices, and customers and did not seek to immediately replace them. Gradually, however, the sales organization will change as more sales people focus on higher-value-added products and services.

Klöckner shows how an interaction field company can be created with simple tools that change the nature of the interactions between the customers and the company. Over time, Klöckner not only transformed its own global organization, but solved problems that transformed the entire steel industry.

If a traditional supply-chain player like Klöckner can rethink and remake the steel industry through the development of an interaction field, any company can do the same in any industry—even one as complex and fraught as health care, as we'll see in the next chapter.

chapter six

Solving Difficult Challenges

Reshaping a Complex Industry

Of all the complex industries we deal with—banking, education, manufacturing, government—health care is probably the most fraught. It has numerous stakeholders, all with different roles and interests, and a highly fragmented system offering services that most people would like to avoid altogether. Not only that, there is little coordination among the various elements.

If only an interaction field company could be built in this industry—if there could be collaboration, interaction, and sharing of data rather than confusion, opacity, and fragmentation. If only regulation wouldn't further complicate matters. The potential of better outcomes, lower costs, and better health care for everyone would be well worth every effort.

In this chapter, I introduce two companies—Discovery Health, a South African insurer, and Flatiron Health, a New York start-up—that have taken on the challenge. They have built interaction fields by sharing data and connecting many participants along the health-care spectrum. These firms' efforts and successes show that interaction field companies can create better outcomes for individuals with a broad range of needs, ultimately saving lives. These companies have also tackled some major challenges in health care, such as the rising costs of personalized clinical therapeutic processes. Most importantly, perhaps, they show that interaction field companies can achieve outcomes in complex, life-and-death industries that no other business model can.

Meet Liam Muller. He lives in Cape Town, South Africa, where he works as an air traffic controller. Liam did a four-year training course and now, years later, is ensconced in his position at the Cape Town International Airport, the second busiest airport in South Africa (after Johannesburg's O. R. Tambo airport). It's one of the better-paying jobs in the area, and Liam takes home around $30,000 annually.

The air traffic controller's life is both stressful and, for the most part, sedentary, and Liam is well aware of the challenges of staying healthy and keeping fit, in both body and mind. In 2015, as Liam turned forty-seven and began to look at age fifty, he decided he needed a new approach to his health and wellness regime. He joined the Vitality health insurance program offered by Discovery Limited, a financial services company providing health, life, home, and car insurances, as well as investment and credit services.

Vitality was built on a simple idea: people could be incentivized to lead healthier lifestyles, which would in turn create a more sustainable insurance market, and, in the long run, benefit society as a whole. This is a very different approach than that of the typical health insurance company. UnitedHealth, Aetna, and all the other monster health insurance providers make the right kind of noises about health and wellness, offering tips on nutrition and exercise and the like, but largely they are in a competitive context, where providing care while relentlessly reducing costs is the game. Health insurance is a highly commoditized market. Payers like Aetna have few ways to differentiate themselves from other providers and therefore can't demand a price premium for better services.

The relationship between the insurance company and service providers, such as hospitals or physicians, is largely transactional. Providers are expected to deliver the minimum standard of care to the insured, while payers try to improve their business performance, which usually means lowering costs or increasing efficiency. But providers want to do more than the minimum. They care about their patients and their professional reputations. They have a calling and a mission to treat and care for patients the best they can, and that includes patients who have limited resources and may not be able to pay for treatment.

Another key participant in the health-care system is the pharmaceutical companies. These guys invest massively in the development of new drugs, a process that can drag on for many years. When they hit the jackpot with a blockbuster drug, they want to recoup their investment as quickly as possible—especially considering that they will have a limited window of exclusivity before the drug goes generic. Insurers, however, are constantly looking to reduce the cost of medications and treatments. Patients are caught in the middle. Insurance premiums keep rising and, if customers want to keep reasonably decent coverage, they have to pay up. If they get sick or need treatment of some kind, they will pay more.

Discovery is different. It has created an interaction field enterprise in one of the most fraught industry sectors on the planet. Unlike the other industries we have looked at here, health care is an industry in which consumers—the nucleus participants—have long been among the most unheard and powerless participants of any industry. Each individual enters the health insurance industry with a unique "background"—genetic programming, medical history, health-related goals and anxieties—to a find a market perplexingly numb to the individual customer, notoriously rigid in structure, and impenetrably opaque in practice. Individuals must learn which doctors are in the network and which are not, which procedures are covered to what amount and which are not, what treatments can be administered and by whom (some in the doctor's office but some at the pharmacy). If there is an error or a disagreement, the insured must prepare for battle and long hours on the telephone with agents and representatives—a phone call that is inevitably followed by a survey. Each month, the mailbox is stuffed with paper statements, envelopes ominously marked IMPORTANT INFORMATION ABOUT YOUR HEALTH COVERAGE, or the like. Within can be found page after page of information about coverages, benefits, charges, contributions of various payers, legalese, and marketing messages. None of this is good for the blood pressure.

The health-care consumer is relatively stuck and powerless. Unlike farmers, who have many choices in equipment suppliers, or construction companies, which can choose from hundreds of steel providers, the health-care patient must apply and be accepted for coverage. They must renew their coverage each year and have little leverage regarding price. They can be rejected for coverage altogether or their claims can be denied. The markets are essentially cornered, monopolized, and exploited. So, while there may be many health-care providers, insurance plans, benefits packages, and doctors and hospitals available, somehow the relationship between health-care provider and insured feels rather like that of warden and prisoner. It doesn't matter much which retail shop you buy your leggings from, but your choice of doctor, hospital, or medication can result in serious—even fatal—outcomes.

Given the widespread awareness of this situation, the industry devotes a good deal of energy to pretending it cares about the individual participant, but rarely offers meaningful ways for customers to provide input. Doctors are famously poor listeners, as we can witness by the amount of literature and consultancies devoted to correcting the problem. (Titles include *When Doctors Don't Listen* and *Patient Listening*.) Nor is there really any way for consumers to regularly and meaningfully participate in their care, their insurance, or the system. Doctors rarely ask you how you would like them to run their practice. Hospitals sometimes look for feedback, but I can't think of many examples of a hospital making improvements in response to customer participation.

There is another aspect of the health-care industry that represents an enormous and largely untapped opportunity for development: data. Health care runs on data; doctors and hospitals collect massive amounts of it from patients, but much of it is siloed, residing on different systems and inaccessible to patients. Data collection, access, and sharing have improved in the past few years. Some doctors and hospital networks now use platforms that enable sharing across practices, disciplines, and facilities, but there are still gaps and inconsistencies in the way data is managed and distributed. If you move from one network to another, or from one geographical location to another, or see specialists who are out of network, it may be difficult to access vital data.

If any industry is begging for an interaction field approach and the inherent shift of attention to the individual participant, it is health care.

The industry is, at least theoretically, united around a common purpose: to promote health, to alleviate pain, to cure illness and avoid disease, and to prolong an insured person's lifespan. This gargantuan industry depends on coordination among several fields, institutions, and entities of various kinds: health and life insurance agencies, hospitals and medical practices (including within public universities), doctors and nurses, patients, specialists, policy makers, equipment and device makers, pharmaceutical companies, mental health providers, physical therapists, and others. The scope is massive! Wouldn't it be fantastic to feel like a participant in one's health and in the improvement of the industry? Wouldn't it be a relief if we felt that our health, the company's well-being, and the fitness of society were somehow aligned?

Fortunately for patients, the industry, and society as a whole, some enterprises are making headway in this direction, including the two whose stories I want to tell: Discovery's Vitality wellness program and Flatiron Health, a data-driven enterprise to cure cancer.

Liam Joins Vitality

Vitality bills itself to insurers as a health and wellness program that offers "a great way to reduce chronic health risks" and to "decrease healthcare costs" while increasing plan membership and improving client retention. Vitality claims to bring "successful, lasting change" to members' health by using "behavioral economics and actuarial science to create effective engagement strategies and compelling incentives that drive long-term behavior change and real business results."

Liam Muller decided that the system sounded promising, and he soon immersed himself in the program, which is organized around a four-phase process: assess, improve, track, reward. Liam's first interaction was a health risk assessment, which included a biometric screening. According to the US Centers for Disease Control and Prevention, this involves the "measurement of physical characteristics such as height, weight, body mass index, blood pressure, blood cholesterol, blood glucose, and aerobic fitness tests," which can be used as part of a "health assessment to benchmark and evaluate changes in employee health status over time."[1] Liam's results showed that he was a bit overweight and had elevated blood pressure, high cholesterol, and rising blood glucose. Not bad, but not great. He did better on the fitness tests. Oh, and he smoked for several years in his twenties before quitting on his thirtieth birthday.

From this data, Liam's "Vitality age" was calculated. This is essentially a risk-adjusted age that is determined by an evaluation of Liam's statistics and readings, which are compared with a massive data resource. At forty-seven, Liam was less than delighted to learn that his Vitality age was fifty-five. He had always considered himself quite healthy and prided himself on his exercise routine, which included biking, recreational football, golf, and walking in the many national parks in Cape Town. He was surprised to learn that he was not quite as healthy as he had assumed.

As much as Liam's Vitality age shocked him, it also motivated him— and this is what Vitality counts on. It was then up to Liam to create a Vitality Personal Pathway, a personalized program of activities and actions to achieve defined goals. For Liam, the goals included modest weight loss, reducing alcohol consumption, more aerobic exercise, incorporating stress-reducing practices, and taking medication to lower his cholesterol.

Vitality borrows from platform companies by offering a rewards system. The more you stick to your program, the more you realize your goals, the more points you receive. Accumulated points earn Vitality Bucks, which can be converted to retail gift cards, a discounted price on an Apple Watch, and more.

Discovery was founded in South Africa in 1992 as a start-up insurance provider but transitioned to an interaction field company by addressing the industry's overarching challenge: How do we make people healthier?

Discovery's innovation was born of necessity. Adrian Gore, Discovery's founder and CEO, says that postapartheid South Africa faced a number of serious challenges, particularly in health care. "There was an undersupply of doctors, an unusual combination of disease burdens, and a new regulatory environment that had zero tolerance for the discrimination of the past, and rightly so. This meant you couldn't rate customers on preexisting conditions." South Africa created a unified, national public health insurance system to take on some of the risk, but many people chose to purchase higher-quality, expensive private insurance.[2] In this challenging context, Discovery and Gore saw opportunity. Gore recalls that the pivotal moment arrived in the company's early days, when a membership-based gym chain approached them with an idea to sell Discovery's health insurance to members. The breakthrough came, Gore writes, when they "flipped this idea around." What if you could earn points for doing things that contribute to good health? And what if those points gave you access to "cool rewards" and a discount on your premiums? Instead of the gym selling its members Discovery's health insurance, why shouldn't Discovery sell its policyholders a gym membership?[3]

From this idea sprouted the Vitality concept: reward people for behavior that will improve their long-term health and simultaneously keep costs down—for both Discovery and its policyholders. The concept fundamentally changes the nature of the interaction between the insurance company and the policyholder. In the traditional model, a policyholder thinks of their insurer as a rate setter, treatment arbiter, and invoice sender. The insurer assesses the risk that the person applying for a policy could become sick and require payouts, and then sets the premium accordingly. Once the person is insured and makes a claim, the battle begins about which conditions and services are covered and which are not. The policyholder needs to learn the language of insurance—with its terms like co-pay, reimbursement rates, and allowable charges—from A to Z.[4] There is little transparency into how costs are determined or what options might be available and not much room for negotiation. The statements are voluminous, the calculations almost unfathomable, and the interactions onerous and to be avoided if at all possible.

Discovery set out to change all that. The company would take a science-based, data-driven approach, thinking of the Vitality program as a partner in health care, not a dictator. They sought to create interactions imbued with meaning, value, and reciprocity as they actively encouraged the achievement of the underlying goal: to make individuals healthier, at less expense.

Vitality is based on some fundamental health science. Data shows that three factors—smoking, nutrition, and physical activity—contribute to the four diseases that, combined, cause more than half of all deaths each year: diabetes, cancer, heart disease, and lung disease.

The Vitality program focuses primarily on exercise and nutrition and engages with its nucleus participants directly to encourage them toward better habits, give them ways to monitor their progress, and reward them for results.

This relationship with nucleus members distinguishes Vitality from other health insurance offerings, but it is the ecosystem that makes it really different. Through partnerships and incentive programs, Vitality influences policyholders' behavior. For a nominal membership fee, members can take advantage of a range of options, from additional hospital coverage that avoids the typical out-of-network charges to a number of additional services for mental health, therapies, and dental coverage for which it is hard to get reimbursement with typical insurers in the United States.

The Vitality ecosystem looks nothing like that of the typical insurance company. With most insurers, the ecosystem participants are doctors, hospitals, and other providers under contract by the insurance company. The company may even purchase or merge with one of the ecosystem members, as Aetna did with CVS. The purpose is to squeeze more cost out of the system, gain more control over patients and prescriptions, and achieve higher profits. One way Aetna will do this is by establishing CVS as the "front door" to the health-care system, ostensibly to make life easier for patients. But the real driver is to divert business away from hospitals and into CVS pharmacies and their MinuteClinics to provide care more efficiently and at lower cost.

The Discovery Health ecosystem is much larger and is focused on healthy and active lifestyles rather than sickness. The list of available options for nucleus participants is rich and varied. There are discounts and deals on gym memberships, stop-smoking programs, health-screening services, spas, hotels, food suppliers, nutrition programs, meditation apps, and sports gear such as running shoes, bikes, sports watches, and activity

Get Apple Watch. Get active. Get rewarded.

Introducing Vitality Active Rewards™ with Apple Watch

Vitality Active Rewards gives Vitality members rewards for getting active. Now your employees can get Apple Watch and use it to achieve their Vitality Active Rewards targets. If your employees earn enough Vitality Points™ for workouts, they can reduce their monthly payment or pay nothing.

To learn more, visit VitalityActiveRewards.com.
Terms and conditions apply.

Visit the App Store to download the Vitality Today™ app.

iPhone 5 or later is required to use Apple Watch. Applicable to Apple Watch Sport 38mm.
Apple is not a participant in or sponsor of Vitality Active Rewards. Terms and conditions apply.

Figure 6. Vitality advertising for an Apple Watch
Source: Adapted from Vitality Group Active Rewards with Apple Watch ad.

trackers. Vitality offers 25 percent cash back on healthy food purchases at partner grocery stores. Nike has even created a collection of Vitality-brand accessories. You can earn points for participating in charity runs. Of course, data tracked from fitness devices and store points-of-sale is gathered and uploaded so the member can monitor it closely.

In other words, through its ecosystem, the Vitality interaction field expands across industries and activities, into food, fitness, philanthropy, travel, and mental health. This is different from the conventional health-care system, which is essentially a network of business organizations involved in the delivery of a specific product or service. In this kind of traditional ecosystem, the engagements are transactional and sometimes in conflict with each other. Insurers want to keep costs down, while pharmaceutical companies want to get a return on their investments in research and development. Negative externalities are common. What benefits the insurer and the care provider is likely to cost of the patient. Very little interaction velocity develops.

The Vitality interaction field, by contrast, is a consumer ecosystem in which consumers are active contributors to value creation. Interaction velocity develops because it is in the best interest of every participant.

As Discovery Health has expanded beyond South Africa, this ecosystem approach has served it well. It has established a presence in other countries by bringing in leading insurance companies as partners. The partners can help Discovery build the localized ecosystem much more effectively and quickly than it could on its own. The interaction field looks different in each country, often due to differences in government regulations, but the benefits of higher interaction velocity are realized everywhere.

Market Makers

Most insurance companies have a set of typical market makers. In the United States, the most important market maker is the Food and Drug Administration (FDA). As defined by the FDA, the agency's mission is to protect the "public health by ensuring the safety, efficacy, and security of human and veterinary drugs, biological products, and medical devices; and by ensuring the safety of our nation's food supply, cosmetics, and products that emit radiation." The agency's purview includes tobacco products and medical products, as well as the dissemination of "accurate, science-based information" that citizens "need to use medical products and foods to maintain and improve their health."[5]

This is an important mission, but not every country has an equivalent of the FDA. In South Africa, where Discovery Health originated, the government health agency does not have the resources to act the way the FDA does in the United States. So Discovery plays a role in the country's health care that is quite similar to the one Alibaba plays in Chinese retail: it is developing and improving the entire industry infrastructure in a way that official bodies cannot.

Clearly, then, the Discovery interaction field is seeking to meet a broad range of needs. For the consumer—the nucleus participant—it is helping people live healthier, longer lives. For the industry, it is working to reduce both friction and costs. For the nation, it is contributing to a healthier society.

Liam became very engaged with Vitality, as did many of his colleagues at the airport. As more people joined and got involved with the program, Vitality became an important part of their lives. Teams formed. Competitions developed. People shared data. They set goals for one another. They could make recommendations for rewards. They checked in on the leaderboard to see who was doing what. Best of all, Liam could log on to his personal Vitality page. There, displayed almost exactly like a credit score, was Liam's Vitality age. There is nothing quite like watching yourself grow younger, even if only theoretically—he dropped from fifty-five to fifty and is working to bring it down even more. The more Liam engaged with Vitality, the more points he earned and the more rewards he was entitled to. This was not, by any means, his experience with his previous health insurance provider.

Liam was not alone in his enthusiasm for Vitality or in the frequency of his interactions. He and his fellow members typically had about forty interactions per month with Vitality, more than one a day. For an insurance company, that is almost unheard of. How often do you interact with your insurance provider? More·important than the number is the quality of Liam's interactions with Vitality, which, as I've defined, consists of three characteristics: meaning, value, and reciprocity.

Meaning. Vitality is changing what it means to have insurance, no longer just insuring against sickness but also shaping healthy behavior. Members who interact with Vitality do not do so with trepidation, resentment, confusion, or apprehension. They understand Vitality's purpose and mission and accept that it is beneficial to all participants.

Value. The interactions create value for participants. We can perhaps further parse value to include three elements:

- *New.* The participant has not had access to this kind of value before: to stay healthy, pay less, *and* live longer. The average age of "healthspan" increases. Previously, Liam did not know his Vitality age, nor was he able to see how his actions could positively affect it.
- *Shared.* All participants in the interaction field gain value—members, physicians, companies, and the insurer. That's why Discovery calls it the "shared value" model. The cost for a participant engaged in the Vitality program is 10 to 15 percent lower than for non-engaged, and savings increase because the Vitality interaction field expands rapidly to provide new opportunities for consumers to stay healthy and save money. Studies have also shown that the work productivity of engaged Vitality participants is higher, because, when participants get sick, the more highly engaged return to work faster.
- *Exponential.* Interaction velocity increases across the entire interaction field, and value multiplies exponentially because of the network effect. The more participants join Vitality, the more value is created, because every participant adds to lowering the overall health-care cost.

Reciprocity. Patients voluntarily contribute their data in a quid pro quo. Vitality adds value to their data by making it easily accessible, manipulable, and understandable. Vitality also uses the data to conduct research, establish norms, develop the most effective practices and treatments, and invest in the most effective benefits and rewards.

The more participants give to Vitality, the more they get from it. Data collected between 2011 and 2014 shows that Vitality members with diamond status—the highest level of engagement—saw a 10 percent reduction in hospital admittance in comparison to members with lower engagement. Overall, Vitality members showed greater attention to their health. They signed up for more detection screenings, particularly for cancer—tests that have been shown to reduce the cost of cancer care thanks to early detection. Vitality members also increased the health content of their food purchased at partner grocery stores—rated some

Members
Improved health, better value through improved
price and benefits

Figure 7. The core elements of the Vitality interaction field
Source: Discovery Results and Cash Dividend Declaration Presentation, June 30, 2018.

34 percent higher than their baseline—and a simultaneous decrease of unhealthy food items. When compared to the nonmember population, diamond status members at age sixty-five have a life expectancy of eight years longer, and costs are some 14 percent lower per patient.[6] A study in 2018 conducted by RAND Europe found that Vitality members who tracked their fitness results in the Vitality platform with an Apple Watch averaged a 34 percent increase in sustained physical activity—that's one extra day of physical activity per week—which Discovery estimates "equates to two more years of life on average."[7]

Be healthier, live longer, and reap the rewards. Discovery's Vitality program makes it more affordable for customers to make healthy lifestyle choices, such as belonging to and going to the gym and eating nutritionally rich foods. It's a reciprocal interaction that provides value and meaning: a longer life with fewer incidents of illness and lower health-care costs, for both the insured and the insurer.

From Health to Life

The shared-value model of Vitality—which hinges on interaction quality and addressing multiple and diverse goals from the individual participant up—was, in 2001, scaled to create Discovery Life, a life insurance product available to Discovery Health members at a 30 percent discount.

The idea driving Discovery Life was adopted from Discovery Health. Instead of offering a fixed-rate policy that does not account for behavioral change that improves health and longevity, the life insurance company includes policyholders as partners who are capable of influencing their policy specifications through their behavior.

Despite entering a well-established market of life insurers in South Africa, Discovery Life quickly became the top provider in the country.[8] Discovery has adopted the model for car insurance as well. Vitality Drive incentivizes safe driving behavior with a proprietary vehicle-tracking system that monitors a host of vehicle and driver behaviors, characteristics, and events: accidents, sharp turns, speed, braking patterns, and the like. Policyholders can also earn as much as 50 percent back on their monthly fuel spending when they fill up at partner service stations.

It is Vitality, however—the bedrock platform for incentivizing behavioral change and personal health care—that has generated extraordinary velocity for Discovery and helped it gain presence in the United Kingdom and Australia, in Asia and Europe, and in the United States. It has done so by building its ecosystem and market maker network.

Discovery has partnered with insurance providers in markets outside of South Africa, including John Hancock in the United States, Ping An in China, and Generali (an Italian company) in Europe. Through this expansive ecosystem of insurance providers—which Vitality enlisted as partners in its interaction field rather than as competitors—the Vitality platform engages with nearly ten million people and attracts more than 150,000 new members every month.[9]

Leveraging this incredible velocity, CEO Adrian Gore announced in November 2018 Vitality's commitment to making 100 million people 20 percent more active by 2025.[10] I wouldn't bet against it. When a platform is created or modified to better fulfill a broad range of goals and needs, it achieves velocity through the demand in its interaction field. Vitality created a better way to insure people, and it has revitalized the industry in doing so. The shared-value insurance is the new model, the ecosystem disruptor, which emerged from a combination of two elements: an essential focus on aligning a broad range of goals within the health insurance market, and engaging customers as participants in optimizing the services and products for fulfilling those goals.

When goals align, an interaction field like what Discovery has developed creates a virtuous cycle—a gift that keeps on giving—for everyone involved. A company that engages its interaction field in such a way is capable of the kind of exponential growth that increases its capacity to achieve goals, from an individual losing a few pounds or lowering his cholesterol to a society and world less plagued by cancers and obesity.

Virtuous indeed.

Flatiron Health: To Cure Cancer

Another player in the health-care industry, Flatiron Health, has sought to create an interaction field to achieve a specific purpose: curing cancer. It is an ambitious goal. Men in the United States have, on average, a nearly 40 percent chance of developing cancer in their lifetime, and women have almost the same risk at 37.6 percent. There will be 18.1 million people diagnosed with cancer this year, and 9.6 million people will die.

The health-care industry—including professionals and leaders within governments, hospitals, universities, oncology departments, biotech labs, and pharmaceutical companies—has been working toward this ambitious goal for decades, perhaps since cancer was discovered near the end of the eighteenth century.

Unfortunately, the many players involved have traditionally engaged one another with little or no integration; they work without being incorporated into a structured hierarchy with a common purpose. Oncologists want to treat specific (but widely varying) cancers as they manifest in patients with unique biological considerations. Pharmaceutical companies want to rapidly develop the most effective treatments and get them to market. Laboratories and research institutions need real-world evidence of cancer development and decay to determine underlying causes and make holistic progress toward a cure.

Flatiron Health was established in 2012 to bring the members of this disjointed ecosystem into an interaction field. Participants engage directly with one another on Flatiron's platform, which is powered by a trove of previously uncoordinated and, to a significant degree, uncaptured and unanalyzed oncological data. According to Zach Weinberg, one of Flatiron's cofounders, "We realized there was no easy solution to ensure that researchers and doctors were collaborating by learning from every patient's experience with cancer. . . . A lot of that data was siloed and difficult to access."[11] Flatiron sought to create something like a universal clinical trial—a system by which every cancer patient "participated" in research by having their data collected, aggregated, and analyzed alongside every other patient.[12]

A first major hurdle for Flatiron's platform was identifying, selecting, and acquiring the data required for it to be effective. The sheer quantity of health-care data available around the world is almost unfathomable, estimated to be 2,314 exabytes, which, according to the World Economic Forum, is comparable to "all the written works of humankind, in every known language, 46,280 times over."[13] (*Exa* signifies one billion billions, or one quintillion.) It's hard to imagine how this estimate was even developed.

Moreover, as Flatiron's founders discovered, a vast amount of relevant data had long been scattered, lost, released, or otherwise disconnected, hiding out in sources—such as doctors' notes, lab results, and radiology reports—euphemistically known as "unstructured documents." To try to reclaim some of those tera-, giga-, and petabytes of data, Flatiron employs a platoon of over one thousand "abstractors"—medical and research professionals and associates who do the nitty-gritty work within partnering medical centers to enter the errant data into Flatiron's proprietary platform, OncoCloud.[14]

Though Flatiron's beginnings were not exactly humble—it was largely funded by entrepreneur-founders Zach Weinberg and Nat Turner (also the CEO), who'd sold their previous company, Invite Media, to Google for $81 million—it did achieve tremendous velocity of its own quite quickly.

Flatiron has built an interaction field that has a large ecosystem. The company partners with 265 community cancer clinics and six major academic research centers.[15] Its platform creates an unparalleled (and previously nonexistent) electronic health record (EHR) for two million active patients, or 12.5 percent of all cancer patients diagnosed annually in the United States. The platform is used by 2,500 clinicians in eight hundred "unique sites of care."[16]

The National Cancer Institute is a partner, and fourteen of the fifteen top life-science companies in oncology interact with Flatiron's platform to access "research-grade data" to variously guide and develop their disparate organizational priorities.[17] With this data, companies are able to make better choices about what products and services to develop. As participants engage and collaborate, a company may discover that its drug is more effective in combination with medications and therapies from other members of the ecosystem. This is the future.

Flatiron wouldn't be nearly as effective in solving many challenges in the oncology interaction field if it weren't for the proactive effort and influence of the market makers. These makers include various associations and societies such as the American Society of Clinical Oncology and the American Society of Hematology, as well as international agencies such as the World Health Organization (WHO), but most important is the FDA, which is an influencer that can create value for all. Access to Flatiron's real-world evidence about what works and doesn't work enables the FDA to make better, swifter decisions, which means that drugs may get quicker approval and come to market sooner than they would have in the old days. In the traditional drug development paradigm, it takes an average of thirteen years from start of development to regulatory approval, but Flatiron cuts that to eight years.

Without the active contribution of the market makers, the interaction velocity that powers the virtuous cycle would never develop. As new treatments are discovered that work on certain patients with certain conditions in certain combinations, that knowledge is shared with everyone in the interaction field. There is no waiting for the information to be distributed informally or appear in scholarly journals. As a result, existing treatments can be refined and new ones rapidly developed. The interaction field gains velocity that benefits everyone and addresses the problems associated with oncology at every level.

In 2018, Flatiron was acquired by the pharmaceutical giant Roche—for whom oncology treatments account for 60 percent of annual revenue—for $1.9 billion.[18] Because Flatiron's comprehensive data sets are both "regulator-worthy" and "clinical research–grade," and because their software analytics extract relevant trends and insights, the "real-world evidence" generated by Flatiron is a tremendous boon to a pharmaceutical company such as Roche seeking to fast-track approval and launch of effective cancer treatments.

Clearly, there is value in what Turner and Weinberg created with Flatiron. It's a platform based on the accumulation and processing of previously uncaptured data, operating within an ecosystem of participants that engage with one another in reciprocal, meaningful, and valuable ways—that is, an interaction field.

It is not difficult to imagine how Flatiron, or a similarly purposed company, might expand. Why stop with cancer? As the Flatiron case study instructs, there is massive potential for companies to create interaction fields within the health-care industry, if only by virtue of the volume of data alone. According to the World Economic Forum, by 2020 humanity will possess more health-care data than we have the capability of storing in all the world's aggregated servers today.[19] Synthesizing and aggregating this data in useful, productive, and beneficial ways—so that it can be shared, evaluated, contributed to, learned from, and leveraged by industries, organizations, and individuals—actuates velocity through an interaction field and can provide the kind of industry upheaval and revolution the health-care field desperately needs.

Meeting Goals in a Complex Industry

As the examples of Discovery and Flatiron demonstrate, if you build an interaction field, you can address a broad range of goals and needs simultaneously—including at the individual, industry, and societal levels.

This is in contrast to the typical value-chain or platform approach, which focuses on a single need or want. Uber or Lyft helps you order a car; OpenTable helps you make a reservation at a restaurant. Interaction field companies can address a number of diverse goals, wants, or needs.

The Vitality example, in particular, proves once again that, for industries with a wide range of participants, an interaction field is the best approach. If you build only a digital platform, you may provide some benefit to the nucleus, but you are not really solving all challenges, since you are just creating an efficient exchange between two parties—as we have seen with Uber and Airbnb. If you build an ecosystem, that is still not sufficient. It brings more participants in, of course, but still it does not tackle larger societal problems. If you build an entire interaction field with a nucleus, ecosystem, and market makers and high interaction velocity, you have the chance to achieve all goals of all participants.

In the old value-chain days, this was not really a corporate goal. The purpose was to compete, win, reward shareholders, make money, grow in size, dominate, and endure as long as possible. Today, that's not enough. A company needs to aim beyond its own self-interest.

Discovery has fundamentally changed the way we think about health insurance. Instead of providing a hedge against the risk of sickness, it focuses on health and social benefit. Discovery did not set out to disrupt the insurance industry (that would be the old thinking in the pipeline world). It set out to provide benefit and shared value for all its participants.

An important lesson of these stories is that data and analytics have tremendous power, not just to gain more customers and sell more stuff, but to create value for huge numbers of participants in complex interaction fields. In the case of Discovery Health, the data comes from physicians by way of nucleus participants, the patients.

For Flatiron, the data collected from physicians and care providers (particularly the unstructured data obtained through abstractors) is shared with participants in the ecosystem and market: competitors, pharma companies, and government agencies. The value that is created isn't just about lowering health-care costs or providing access to health-care services for more people; it is about developing entirely new drug treatments, new combinations of drugs, and new therapeutic regimens and services that, if not able to eliminate cancer, enable patients to live a decent life with the disease. It can also be about accelerating drug approval. The likelihood of a person being diagnosed with cancer at some time in his or her life is about 40 percent. More than eighteen million people are diagnosed every year, and more than nine million people die of the disease, so speedier drug approval would be a highly valuable outcome. This kind of value only can be realized by recognizing that the market makers are among the most important participants in the interaction field.

What's particularly appealing about both companies is that the patients—those long ignored, bullied, and mistreated participants like Liam—contribute as much value as they receive. The same is true for participants in business areas where the drivers are quite different. While worry and complexity have long characterized the world of health care, a very different interaction field—created by action camera maker GoPro—is motivated by the joys and thrills of adventure and extreme sports.

chapter seven

The Virtuous Cycle

The Sociology of Gravitational Pull II

I hope it's clear by now that for nearly every industry, the value-chain model is a thing of the past and the platform model is just not enough. You need a nucleus, an ecosystem, and market makers to create an interaction field. You need velocity of interactions to create the most value for all participants within the field and in the larger society.

But every interaction field enterprise is different, and so far we've spent our time looking at large ones that can embrace a huge number and great variety of participants—as is particularly the case with Alibaba and Discovery Health. However, not every interaction field is so broad and complex, and not every field will proliferate with such velocity. That's OK. As we've said, growth is not always about size and quantitative scope.

The action camera maker GoPro is a very different kind of company. It creates interactions with a limited set of participants and a highly focused and narrow interaction field. To get a sense of the advantages and limitations that arise in such a situation, we take a look at how GoPro builds velocity in its interaction field, some missteps it made in trying to expand it, and how it continues to feed the virtuous cycle that keeps the company going.

GoPro has many characteristics that might be associated with a more traditional value-chain start-up. It is the company, after all, that has had tremendous success in the most traditional metric of all: money. GoPro's skyrocketing growth turned founder Nick Woodman into America's youngest billionaire in 2012. When GoPro went public in 2014, it was one of the most successful initial public offerings (IPOs) ever. Thanks to the capital that poured in from the IPO, Woodman became the highest-paid CEO in the United States. At the time, the media predicted that he would be the next Steve Jobs.

Woodman did not exactly take on the mantle of entrepreneur-innovator-genius that Jobs left empty when he died in 2011. Nor did GoPro carry on with its red-hot performance. To some investors and observers, GoPro is now seen as a disappointment. Since going public, management has made mistakes, botched initiatives, and failed to maintain its financial momentum. Today, the share price is near an all-time low and shows little sign of rising.

But that is a rather narrow view of what GoPro has achieved. It has also withstood the efforts of some the most capable companies in the world—including Sony and Apple—to horn in on its territory. Despite mediocre share performance, GoPro has held on to its lead in the action camera market. Most important, from my point of view, it is the only company that has built an enormously committed community of customers around the world and created an interaction field enterprise in a very distinct and constricted market. So while GoPro did make poor decisions about such traditional matters as product development (no company is perfect), I applaud it for expertly developing the velocity that has sustained the company and kept it independent for almost fifteen years.

GoPro provides an interesting example of how to create an interaction field from scratch. It's very different from the process followed by the big, established companies or the start-ups flush with venture funding. Like in any start-up, GoPro has no legacy barriers, no fixed assets to worry about, no brand equity to inhibit its movement. In some ways, creating an interaction field from nothing is easier—if you can stay alive long enough to crank the flywheel of velocity.

To develop velocity, a start-up enterprise like GoPro—with little or modest funding and big dreams—needs to create gravitational pull to attract people to participate. That is the downside of the start-up: there is no customer base, no ecosystem members, and no clearly defined set of market makers. There is no industry knowledge or experience, and no network of long-term collaborations with distribution-channel partners of the kind that camera makers like Sony, Nikon, and Olympus can rely on. It all must be determined as you go, and pulling people into the field is essential to gaining enough velocity and creating a virtuous cycle.[1] To develop velocity is part science and part art, and it requires both persistence and a little luck. The science comes through knowledge of such disciplines as behavioral economics, network theory, social influence theory, social impact theory, and social network analyses. The art is being able to apply the knowledge—skillfully and creatively—to drive interaction velocity.

In 2002, Nick Woodman, age twenty-seven, rounded up a few friends and flew to Australia to surf. By then, he had founded two businesses, both of which went belly-up. He decided he needed to rethink and reset his life. Surfing was the best way he knew to do that.

Woodman loved surfing more than almost anything else. He shared the fleeting moments of bliss with his friends on the waves, but once the moment was over, it was gone. "Some of the most intense and memorable moments in cranking surf were just that, memories," he said later. "Every time one of us would get a sick barrel, we'd say to each other: 'Agghh! If only we had a camera!'" (Getting a barrel is when the surfer slices along roughly parallel to the shore inside the curl of a wave.) Woodman knew that it was only professional surfers who were likely to get a shot of themselves in a sick barrel, because they were sometimes followed by professional photographers who possessed the kind of specialized—and expensive—equipment needed to capture the fast and furious action.

Woodman had been noodling for some time with the idea of a wearable camera that he could take into the surf with him. In Australia, he became obsessed with how to capture those amazing moments on the water. He tried strapping a thirty-five millimeter still camera to his hand with a rubber band, with limited success. The images he could get from the beach with inexpensive equipment did not do justice to the action. It was during that trip that the idea of a portable, "invisible" camera really took hold in Woodman's mind. Looking back to those inspirational days on the water, Woodman said, "I'd kill for some GoPro footage of that trip!"[2]

After his Australian sojourn in 2002, Woodman went home to California and spent the next couple of years working on a camera prototype. He borrowed money from his father, an investment banker, to fund development of the camera and a sewing machine from his mother, so he could mess around with strap design. He plowed about $10,000 of his own money into the idea. That money came from an earlier venture: on a trip to Bali with his girlfriend, Woodman bought a slew of shell necklaces for $1.90 each, then came home to the California coast and sold them out of his Volkswagen bus.

In 2004, Woodman launched the first GoPro camera, again using his VW bus as a retail venue. It was a basic thirty-five millimeter still camera, modified with a leather strap and a rugged housing and sold at a price point most surfers could afford: $20. Cost to make the product in China: $3. With a couple of lucky sales and good exposure, the GoPro took off. By 2012, GoPro was selling more than two million cameras a year. That year, a Taiwanese electronics company, Foxconn, bought an equity stake, making Woodman a paper billionaire. In 2014, the company went public, raised $427 million at a valuation of nearly $3 billion, and Woodman became the highest-paid CEO in the United States.[3]

Along the way, the camera evolved considerably, and today it is a remarkable device with the capacity to capture fast-paced action in all kinds of difficult environments, from rolling breakers to Alpine snowfields. It's a rugged, boxy gizmo with advanced features like image stabilization to smooth out jumpy action and time-lapse capability for longer-duration events such as river rafting. It features voice control for hands-free situations and is waterproof for use in, or under, water. The wind noise reduction feature produces quality sound during cliff jumps, high-altitude skiing, storm surfing, and the like. The camera can be attached to almost anything: a surfboard, ski tip, wingsuit, or skydiver's arm.

GoPro is the aspirational, cool, invisible camera that Woodman envisioned. It enables regular people to get the kind of images that only professionals had been able to capture previously—hence the name GoPro, short for "going professional." It is, to this day, still reasonably affordable, with models starting at $200 and ranging to $600.

If the camera were all we had to talk about with GoPro, its story would not be in this book. The key to GoPro is sharing, and that had largely to do with entrepreneurial luck. As it happened, in February 2005, a year after GoPro launched its first camera, three former PayPal employees created a service called YouTube, which they sold in November 2006 to Google. Woodman had originally conceived of GoPro as a way to capture his sick barrel moments and show them to his surfer friends who were not actually on the water with him—a camera company with a small and finite niche audience. As the camera went from still to video, YouTube was also taking off, and the combination provided a way to share those moments with people anywhere, simply by posting them online for anyone to comment on and share. This enabled GoPro enthusiasts around the world to show up and show off, to exchange knowledge about places and practices, and to challenge one another to new heights of achievement. The GoPro platform enables instant upload of footage to the cloud, download of editing software, and, most important, connection to others in a way that creates interest and value for all.

The camera now can automatically upload and edit pictures and video as soon as it comes close to a WiFi connection, thanks to two software programs, GoPro Studio and GoPro Quik. For example, a surfer might return to shore for a coffee break, and as she approaches the surf shack (there is always a surf shack), the camera uploads the video taken over the last few hours of surfing, without any action needed on her part. The technology automatically selects the best fifteen-second shots from the preceding hours of video, all while the surfer waits for her coffee.

Let's look at GoPro from an interaction field perspective. At the core is the nucleus, which consists of two types of participants. At the beginning, one group was composed of surfers, the creators. They sought to capture and share their moments of achievement or bliss. The other group was made up of spectators, admirers, groupies, wannabes, and someday-will-bes—the consumers, some eighty million of them. Many of them were into surfing, some of them just love extreme sports of any kind.

As GoPro took off, the participants came to include all kinds of adventurers and would-be adventurers, not just surfers. In other words, the nucleus expanded beyond the hard-core surfing community. On GoPro's site, people can upload and watch videos created by GoPro users doing amazing and captivating things: hunting eagles, backcountry skiing in Chile, mountain biking across the Gobi Desert, helicoptering over New York City. It is a community whose members interact, and in which everybody contributes value to the site, the company, and each other.

In order to have maximum reach and create value for the extreme athletes, GoPro has developed a vibrant ecosystem of media partners. These include YouTube, which posts selected images and videos and alerts the major social media channels when new content is available. On YouTube alone, GoPro has some seven million subscribers and approximately two billion views. On all social media platforms, GoPro has over thirty million regular followers based in twenty-two countries. The creators can further share their videos in their own networks. Each video is identified with a GoPro watermark that shows that the video was captured with a GoPro camera.

As viewers share a video of a surfer, for example, all participants and the company benefit. The surfer gets more exposure for her video, while GoPro gets more exposure for its GoPro videos, with potentially new consumers who become motivated to purchase a GoPro camera themselves. It is a virtuous cycle—from image capture to equipment purchase—that gains velocity as more consumers post, share, and comment.

GoPro participants become powerful brand builders. They post their exploits at the rate of about six thousand pieces of content a day, and

Figure 8. The GoPro virtuous cycle
Source: GoPro Investor Presentation, 2016.

GoPro amplifies their images, videos, and content on social channels including YouTube. This makes the content available to a wider social network.

More than one million people have used the hashtag #GoPro to upload footage. Such high velocity in the GoPro interaction field is not a coincidence. GoPro actively manages it. There are close connections and mutual exchanges between GoPro and professional photographers, surfers and other action sports athletes, and brand ambassadors and influencers. GoPro sponsors over one hundred forty athletes, which supplements their incomes (sometimes quite meager) and gives them remarkable access to millions of fans. GoPro, in turn, gets access to images of the athletes' high-energy lives and adrenaline-fueled exploits in locations from the highest peaks to the ocean floor. Some of the athletes are already celebrities, such as the three-time Olympic gold medal snowboarder Shaun White, surfing legend Kelly Slater, and Jimmy Chin, a professional climber and photographer with over two million Instagram followers. Others include big mountain skier Chris Davenport, snowboarder Travis Rice, and trials cyclist Danny MacAskill.

GoPro also manages a standout brand ambassador program. Anyone can sign up on the website to be an ambassador. Ambassadors are encouraged to post their own stills or videos, which can win as the best of the day and may get them into the GoPro best of the year competition. They can win cash prizes ranging from $50 to $5,000.

GoPro organizes numerous events where like-minded photographers, artists, athletes, and other enthusiasts come together. The Gold Coast event, held in Australia, is for serious GoPro members who are addicted to the extreme-sports lifestyle: surfing the big waves, skydiving, freestyle ski acrobatics, rock climbing, you name it.

If you qualify as a macro-influencer—a participant with a huge social media following—GoPro bestows a camera upon you so you can record your crazy adventures. All you are asked to do is transmit the content back to home base whenever you get a moment off piste. A team of GoPro video producers and photographers packages the incoming content and uploads it to one of the channels. If you are micro-influencer, which means you have a few thousand followers, you can still sign up on the GoPro site and get access to the community. (I am a micro, but I'm working on it.)

One of the most important participants in the GoPro ecosystem is the energy drink Red Bull. The two brands fit together like the front and back of the same page. They both appeal to the same types of people. They both explicitly endorse and encourage an aspirational lifestyle filled with action, adventure, memorable experiences, and living on the edge. What edge that is, you choose. Red Bull does GoPro a huge service by extending its reach to the more than 170 countries where the energy drink is available. Red Bull conducts events in many of those countries, and GoPro is always there. Many key figures in culture, arts, music, and dance also use GoPro without any formal connection or endorsement.

GoPro makes these investments to build awareness, attract participants, enhance the richness of the brand, and drive traffic to the thousands of retail sites where GoPro products are sold. Since social media is an exponential technology that builds on the network effect, GoPro benefits exponentially as well. The strategy pulls in the many kinds of participants who use GoPro cameras for special purposes, such as the US military, police forces, rock bands, and professional sports teams.

Around 2016, GoPro made a major strategy change. It decided that it wanted to break out of the narrow market of extreme sports and appeal to a broader audience. GoPro thought that many more people should use the cameras for more mundane purposes, such as family snapshots and Instagram posts, thus enlarging the scope of the nucleus. Strap the camera on the handlebars of a kid's bike or the collar of the family dog, and you're likely to get some post-able, shareable shots. The idea was that GoPro should be a little bit more everyday, a little more relevant to people who did not prefer to live at the bleeding edge of activity. GoPro quickly learned, however, that people did not really require an action camera to record birthday parties, bike trips to the pool, or romping dogs. For that, the cell-phone camera was more than adequate.

The initiative did not do GoPro any good, because it fuzzed the definition of the true nucleus participant. The images of family outings, kids on bikes, and cats on roofs actually had a negative effect on the images of daring adventurers clinging to cliffsides and leaping from airplanes. It weakened the network effect. Family pictures might be highly valuable to a close-knit group but not at all to a larger audience. Did GoPro really think that the dude with the jelly-roll belly was equivalent to Jimmy Chin? In 2017, GoPro saw that the expansion plan was ill-advised. As Nick Woodman put it, "What we've learned ultimately is that not everybody needs a GoPro. We don't need to make GoPro relevant to everybody to be successful."[4]

There were other missteps. At one point, GoPro began to think of itself as a producer of original content and invested in making documentaries and TV-like series. That venture failed. It is likely that the participants in the GoPro interaction field thought of themselves as better content producers than GoPro the company, whose action shots could be perceived as staged or produced. GoPro also invested in related products, such as drones, but could not compete with companies offering better technology faster and cheaper.

Through it all, GoPro has managed to steadily build velocity and maintain its virtuous cycle. Without it, the company could not have survived a concerted effort by Apple, Sony, and ultracompetitive Chinese company DJI to seize the market. GoPro remains the undisputed leader. That's because the other companies could not reproduce, or match for richness and velocity, GoPro's interaction field.

In Chapter 4, I talked about two factors that create gravitational pull. The first was framing, and we saw how LEGO's framing has had a significant impact on interaction velocity. The same is true with GoPro. The second factor is the connectivity of the participants in the interaction field. These two factors are intimately linked. GoPro's framing is defined in its mission statement: "Helping people capture and share their lives' most meaningful experiences with others—to celebrate them together." The framing helps to build velocity because it focuses on the sharing part of the camera experience, rather than on the individual's goal of capturing the perfect shot. The focus on sharing encourages connecting; celebrating together requires interactivity. The second factor, connectivity, guarantees strong gravitational pull. Typically, large and close-knit communities (aka tribes) have already formed around the kind of high-action sports that are so much a part of GoPro: snowboarding, surfing, BMX biking, and so on. The members of these groups are usually highly engaged with each other in various ways—either through one-on-one communication or live get-togethers—so they are ready for online interactivity and eager to share content more widely. In short, with GoPro, the motivation of the target consumers, the strong ties among them, and the intelligence they share are important contributors to GoPro's success in building an interaction field with high velocity.

But those are not the only factors that contribute to gravitational pull.

Gravitational Pull: Sharing Factors

People choose to participate in an interaction field for many reasons. Malcolm Gladwell wrote about the reasons in the *New Yorker* article that was the basis of his best-selling book *The Tipping Point*.[5] He provided a comprehensive summary of the science behind sharing and spreading of ideas, and he identified three sets of factors or characteristics:

- *The law of the few.* Gladwell defines a set of factors that make people influential. He suggests that a small number of these influential people are responsible for creating virality. He argues that about 20 percent of the "carriers" of an idea cause 80 percent of "infections." He identified three types of carriers:
  - › connectors, who have massive social networks with many acquaintances;
  - › salesmen, who boast about ideas they love and who are highly contagious; and
  - › mavens, who gather information, serve as a resource for others, and share knowledge.
- *The stickiness factor.* Gladwell discusses content factors associated with the idea or message that indicate how likely it is to be shared. These factors have been further elaborated on by others over the years.[6]
- *The power of context.* Gladwell describes a set of environmental factors that contribute to the dissemination of ideas. He argues that small environmental details can have an impact on people's behaviors.

In terms of specific sharing of content, knowledge, data, and information by consumers and brands, I have conducted over fifty thousand consumer interviews across several hundred brands in more than twelve countries between 2009 and 2016.[7] When a company or brand has consumers that are willing to share content about it, that company has social currency, a term I first coined in 2009.[8]

My research shows that there are seven factors that determine consumers' willingness to share content about a brand or company. The more consumers share, the more the brand becomes part of their lives, the more it fits into their daily schedules, and the higher the degree to which they are willing to share additional information and data with others. These factors include:

- *Personal identity.* People share with brands depending on how much the relationship with the brand plays into their self-image. For extreme sports people, having a much-liked video on the GoPro channel reflects well on them and helps them identify with a particular extreme sport.
- *Social identity.* This is the sense of belonging or kinship with others who use a brand or product. While the need for expressing community within a family is very high, the size of the family is rather limited, and hence there is relatively little sharing of GoPro videos or photos. In contrast, the motivation to express allegiance to a group in a particular extreme sport means the audience is much larger.
- *Expression.* The more a brand facilitates my need to communicate who I am, the more I am willing to share. GoPro facilitates social expression for a person because the company uploads a constant stream of the best GoPro clips from user-submitted videos.
- *Conversation.* People are more likely to participate when they feel emotional about or connected to the activity that engages them. The GoPro videos can be beautiful, inspiring, nerve-racking, even funny (check out the video in which a seagull snatches a GoPro in its beak and takes off).[9]
- *Affiliation.* The more a brand, product, or service helps a consumer to forge new social connections or relationships, the more its content will be shared. GoPro empowers its users to connect with other athletes.
- *Utility.* People want to help each other, teach each other, and solve problems for and with each other, and they are looking for brands to help them. GoPro videos contain a lot of information and practical advice about a huge range of activities. If you want to learn how to BASE jump off a cliff in your wingsuit, for example, it's all there within the GoPro field.

- *Information.* People seek out people and brands that help them discover new things. GoPro is all about discovery. In the videos that people share, we see others' experiences of travel, adventure, relationships, mishaps, and achievements.

How to Build Gravitational Pull That Powers the Interaction Field and Virtuous Cycle

Over the last several years, there has been a proliferation of new platforms and digital ecosystems. Many will fail; consulting firm Accenture estimates that only about 10 percent will survive.[10] There are many reasons why a business fails, but for platforms, digital ecosystems, and interaction fields, an important reason is if they haven't created a gravitational pull that feeds the virtuous cycle. It is extremely difficult to create this pull for any company—large or small, pipeline or start-up. It is the classic *chicken-and-egg strategy* problem: How do you get the network effect started when you don't have participants or users? And, relatedly, how do you virally attract new participants when you have no participants to create the virality? It is the toughest challenge that any business ever faces.

I believe that the best way to solve this challenge is to understand really, really well how gravitational pull is created toward the nucleus of the interaction field. I have already discussed what is required. There are three major factors, two of which I outlined in Chapter 4: framing and branding, and connecting with others. The third factor is what makes people want to share something about a company or brand with others, as discussed earlier.

What, then, are the steps that you need to take to make gravitational pull happen?

STEP 1: Define what you are solving for and how you fit into the world of participants in the interaction field

You must be clear about the purpose of your interaction field. Framing it from a traditional perspective will not be effective, as we have seen throughout the book. The logical point of departure is to frame the interaction field from the consumers' challenges or perspective. Fortunately, the frameworks, models, and approaches to do that are already well established.[11]

One way to start is to break down the life of a GoPro surfer into "dayparts" or minutes. There are 1,440 minutes in a surfer's typical day. Consider a fictional surfer, German Yunes, who starts his day checking out the waves in Punta del Este, Uruguay, where he lives. He paddles out, catches a few waves, comes ashore for breakfast, then hangs out with friends. After a simple lunch, there is an obligatory nap. The waves pick up later as the sun sets over the ocean, and Yunes is back at it. He finishes for the day and runs a few errands in town before going out for dinner.

The research process involves defining the activities and goals of surfers like Yunes for each of the dayparts. This can involve studying a few consumers in-depth, using ethnographic-inspired methods, or a large sample of consumers using a survey. Today it is typical to ask several hundreds of consumers to track their activities with their mobile devices. Consumers are instructed to capture and record moments of their lives, and then these moments can be further elaborated on by soliciting consumer stories. This helps researchers to understand the context of use and consumption. The data can be analyzed and grouped into clusters, or mega-moments, of interest. A food company might be interested in any food consumption during the day and likely will zoom in on the moments that are associated with consuming food or drinks.

It is helpful to project these moments into the future to understand how the daily life of a surfer changes over the years and how needs evolve. A researcher might consult with experts in technology, consumer culture, urban planning, and sociology to understand how aspects of consumers' lives change over time, in regard to finances, eating, entertaining, and mobility and transportation.

The goal is to create future life maps of surfers that can then be used to learn about the problems, challenges, pain points, and jobs to be done in the future. As early as 2004, for example, it was clear that surfers' photos were shared online, using software such as EasyShare by Kodak. By analyzing technology trends such as the increase in broadband capabilities, it would have been possible for GoPro to evaluate a near-future situation where people could upload entire videos to a site and share them across computers—the technology that essentially became YouTube. By creating future life maps, it is possible to better understand the contexts, capabilities, and challenges that make up the life of a surfer several years out, as well as the implications for creating and designing an interaction field.

STEP 2: Identify the participants that create value among the nucleus, ecosystem, and market makers and analyze their core interactions

This step requires understanding the motivations of the potential participants and the connections among them. One way to do this is through participant mapping, a workshop process that can determine the participants in the nucleus, ecosystem, and market makers that either have significant influence on others or contribute or receive value from others.

This is important because you do not always know who the direct participants in the nucleus are and how they connect with one another. With Uber, for example, riders don't really care about who else is using Uber or who the drivers are. In the GoPro market, however, surfers care a lot about who else is posting. They recognize the influencers and follow the celebrities who are part of the GoPro ecosystem. Hence it is important to analyze the influence that participants have on each other.

This is fundamentally different from the typical pipeline-company approach to consumer research, in which consumers are grouped by one or more characteristics: demographics, lifestyle, or psychographics and need states. This is known as market segmentation. In order to build an interaction field, it is more appropriate to segment people in terms of influence or connectivity—that is, the number of links they have with others. GoPro could segment their participants by relative activity, power, and influence on interaction velocity.

GoPro also needs to determine the ecosystem participants who contribute value to the nucleus participants: the companies that provide accessories and associated products for GoPro cameras. And it should study the market makers that influence the velocity. Over twenty-five million

GoPro cameras have been shipped over the last five years, while the potential number of users is estimated north of eighty million. As these users become part of the nucleus, they create velocity.

One useful exercise is to study the linkages and connections of influencers. They could be macro-influencers like Lakey Peterson, a well-known professional surfer in the World Surf League and a GoPro ambassador. Or they could be micro-influencers or even nano-influencers (people who have very few followers but have a strong influence on potential consumers). It is helpful to think of influence in terms of relevance, reach, and resonance. Shaun White would score high on relevance to snowboarders, and he reaches a global audience because of his success in the Olympic Games. He also has resonance because he engages with audiences involved in a number of other activities, such as skateboarding and music.

STEP 3: Make it easy to participate and share

It is helpful to understand how people currently go about solving the problem you have identified. For example, GoPro could study how a beginner surfer learns about the various types of surfing conditions and waves he is likely to encounter, such as reef breaks, point breaks, or reform breaks. The surfer might engage in search and research activities (asking friends, going online), discovery (watching GoPro videos), comparing (studying alternative pro surfers), practicing, getting help (asking other surfers in a forum), sharing, and evangelizing. To understand how the surfer solves the problem of learning, you can employ a journey-mapping process, which shows where and at what point a participant should be encouraged to join in, and how many reinforcements will be necessary to create sufficient gravitational pull. When properly done, a journey map describes every step of an experience—such as learning about various surf waves—from the participant's perspective in terms of doing, thinking, feeling, and the overall experience.

In the pipeline world, a company or brand would go about this from a touch-point perspective. An automotive company might ask, "What is the set of touch points where I connect with a potential new car buyer?" The touch points might be watching TV, visiting a website, reading a magazine, or visiting a dealership. In understanding these touch points, the pipeline company's goal is to communicate the brand consistently at each one. Today, this approach has its problems. There are so many digital touch points, as many as nine hundred in the process of buying a car. Each of these can become an opportunity to engage with a potential car buyer and each can be an opportunity for the buyer to share the brand. Each can also be a hazard, in which the brand may be presented in a negative light or inconsistently.

It can be necessary for a company to go through extraordinary efforts to make it easy to participate and share. In Chapter 6, I described Flatiron Health. The founders of this company believed that if they could organize the cancer treatment data from millions of patients—and make the data easy to aggregate, analyze, and generate insights from—they could improve patient outcomes. The challenge was that most of the patient and treatment data was not recorded, and what was available was unstructured and difficult to work with. The solution was to hire several thousand medical abstractors, individuals who followed doctors at cancer hospitals and collected the clinical data. Machine learning and artificial intelligence software was used to organize this data and combine it with claims data, genomic data, and mortality data. Then all of it was made available to patients, providers, payers, pharmaceutical companies, regulators, and cancer institutions. Flatiron Health also had to build software products to make it easy for doctors, hospitals, and care centers to share the data.

STEP 4: Define what kind of value will be created for all participants in the interaction field

Most businesses fail not because they don't have a great product, but because they don't consider what value they create for all the relevant participants in their interaction field. GM built an electric car long before Elon Musk hit on the idea of Tesla. GM spent over a billion dollars developing the EV1 and tried to market it through its dealer network. The cars did not sell, and GM concluded that there wasn't enough of a market for electric cars beyond the relatively small number of environmentalists and tech enthusiasts. But the real reason the cars did not sell was that the dealers did not want to sell them. They would go so far as to take delivery of the electric vehicles (EVs) but not display them. This was because the cars were not good for the dealers' lucrative maintenance and repair businesses. Electric cars have fewer mechanical parts than gas-powered ones and rarely break down. Dealers make most of their money on servicing, repairing, and maintaining vehicles, so electric cars would seriously cannibalize that business. In short, GM did not consider how to create value for one of its major and most important ecosystem participants: dealers.

GoPro built software technology to make it easy for users to post content. The company gives out prizes for best content, organizes awards celebrations, and established GoPro Studio so users could edit their own video content. Such actions create value for the user who seeks attention, fame, or reputation among the community of surfers, or, sometimes, from an even wider audience.

MoviePass was a subscription-based movie ticketing service that offered participants a daily discounted movie ticket, for available shows, for less than $10 per month. Moviegoers loved the service. Movie-theater owners did not. MoviePass tried to convince them that the increased volume of attendees at off-peak showtimes would enable the theater to sell more than enough drinks, candy, and popcorn to make up for the discounted ticket price. The theaters did not buy it. The service eventually went out of business.

The key to success in building an interaction field where participation and sharing drives interaction velocity is to build a system that creates value through collaboration and coordination for all participants.

If you look at GoPro as a business, you would be forgiven if you were to call it a consumer electronics company. On the GoPro site, there is an extensive line of cameras and accessories available and plenty of promotional content about how these are the world's most versatile action cameras. The core product, the HERO8, is the company's best camera to date and quickly fueled speculation about what new capabilities the HERO9 will offer.

Yet GoPro's success has as much to do with the company's ability to build and nurture an interaction field as it does with its ability to relentlessly innovate, and there are three major factors that influence its virtuous cycle: framing, connectivity, and sharing. These factors apply across the entire interaction field: the nucleus, the ecosystem, and the market makers.

Market makers have a particular role in feeding the virtuous cycle because they influence the velocity. Market makers can be any type of participant—a potential consumer, an institution like the FDA, or a competitor, as in Tesla and Volkswagen. One of Tesla's competitive advantages is its electric vehicle charging station network, consisting of more than 1,500 Supercharger stations worldwide, which work only for Tesla cars. But Tesla owners can also charge their cars at a number of other charging stations, such as those from Volkswagen, which is installing charging stations in major cities throughout the world. Because range matters for EVs, Volkswagen is a market maker for Tesla, influencing the adoption of Tesla cars. The US government, which funds agriculture to the tune of $20 billion a year, is a market maker for John Deere.

The challenge is that market makers don't benefit the same way as participants in a platform business or digital ecosystem. This is particularly so when market makers are new consumers. They benefit only indirectly, while platform participants and ecosystem participants benefit directly. Consumers that are not part of GoPro benefit from the entertainment value of the videos created by participants showing off their latest adventures. That's a different benefit from the one that GoPro camera users get by watching videos to learn new tricks.

GoPro shows that it is necessary to recognize the power of market makers and design ways to attract them, so as to accelerate velocity. As we'll see in the next chapter, this activity becomes more complicated in industries that are characterized by constant flux, frequent breakthroughs in technology, shifting customer behavior, and, as a result, one disruption after another. Such is the world of mobility, where designing an interaction field involves placing bets on the future evolution of technology, business, and society.

chapter eight

Superfluid Markets

Eliminating Frictions

It's hard to build an interaction field in any industry, but it is especially difficult in an industry that is in constant flux. When you are part of such a market, it's tough to see the opportunities for eliminating frictions. To do so, it's necessary to take a step back and try to get some perspective. As Xerox PARC researcher and computer pioneer Alan Kay put it, "Perspective is worth eighty IQ points.[1]

Just as all interaction fields are not the same, the markets and industries in which they operate are all quite different. One way to think about them is in terms of fluidity. A superfluid market is characterized by rapid change and extreme shifts in market dynamics, driven by changing consumer expectations, emerging competitors, and novel and disruptive technologies. Many markets touched by the Internet—such as bookselling, newspapers, and advertising—have experienced superfluidity, which caused categories and industries to readjust and reorganize.

A good example of a superfluid market today is the automotive industry. It is in the midst of multiple disruptions and is reshaping itself in many ways—all in plain sight. As Toyota president Akio Toyoda said, "The automotive industry is now hurtling into an era of profound transformation, the likes of which come[s] only once every 100 years. With even our rivals and the rules of competition also changing, a life-or-death battle has begun in a world of unknowns."[2]

Some observers believe this profound change and industry havoc is created by technology-driven companies—such as Tesla, Waymo, and Uber—that have forced incumbents to become providers of mobility services. But the real driver is the technologies themselves, not so much the disruptor companies. We are seeing the emergence, convergence, and refinement of several new technologies that underlie the changes—including autonomous driving, electrification, e-mobility (such as car- and ride-sharing), and connectivity (principally because of GPS). Other new technologies such as machine learning, AI, and robotics, while not directly associated with mobility, are maturing and will have an impact on every part of the traditional automotive value chain, provoking change in the structure of the industry and the nature of competition within it.

In previous chapters, we have discussed the challenges involved in creating an interaction field company, and you may have the impression that it takes enormous effort, a great deal of talent, and a lot of good luck to succeed. Klöckner, for example, had to deal with a fragmented market, and GoPro needed to develop velocity with a relatively limited set of participants. But neither the metals industry nor the action camera category operates within a superfluid market. They have been affected and changed by technology, for sure, but the basic industry structure remains in place. Consumer expectations rise and competition intensifies, but the dynamics do not fundamentally change. The automotive industry, by contrast, is in constant flux—it is superfluid.

The question, then, is how to build an interaction field that harnesses the energy of the change taking place in a superfluid market.

STEP 1: Identify the market's major frictions, strains, or inefficiencies

One way to do this is to look at each layer: from the individual driver, owner, or person seeking transportation, to the frictions or inefficiencies in the industry, to the strains on society overall. Once identified, break them down into the individual parts. At the industry level, for example, components would include mining, materials, assembly, retail, repair and service, scrap, waste, and so on. Then, look at the major frictions between the various segments—for example, specifying, ordering, shipping, handling, disposal, and recycling.

Another approach is to look at the industry from the perspective of the consumer. Today, a consumer, on average, engages in more than nine hundred digital interactions while buying a car. So we can start with deconstructing the steps and individual experiences involved, analyzing the frictions from the point of view of potential participants. What are the specific engagements required to obtain financing, select and buy insurance, join an automobile association, register the car, arrange for parking, find a mechanic, and on and on? The consumer may encounter friction of various kinds at any or all of these points along the journey. For example, I may feel friction when the products that are available, and that I have the capacity to buy, rub up against the intellectual, social, and emotional pressures I feel as I try to adhere to an environmentally responsible lifestyle. Can I really buy that Lamborghini, given the current discussion on global warming? Out of the question!

STEP 2: Define the technologies that solve the frictions, strains, and inefficiencies that matter

More often than not, these will be emerging technological capabilities or platforms—for example, autonomous driving or electric cars. The key is to assess how the technology facilitates voluminous and rapid interactions among the components of the industry ecosystem and how it can power the nucleus of an interaction field enterprise.

STEP 3: Monitor and evaluate the impact of reducing or eliminating the frictions

Do it for each layer: consumers, the industry, or society in general. Identify opportunities for velocity within the superfluid market.

STEP 4: Envision the role of the company in evolving toward an interaction field company

This means identifying places where frictions will be smoothed or eradicated and designing the business to perform that function first, while maintaining an industry-wide view in which new opportunities can be adapted to and drawn in by gravitational pull.

Keep in mind that the opportunity is not only about ensuring a sustainable business and effectively competing in a changing market, but also about solving some of the societal challenges of our times, because automobiles and transportation affect every part of consumers' lives.

So, the automotive industry—which has been subsumed into the mobility arena—is perhaps the most familiar example of a superfluid market. It has always been a business ecosystem with multiple participants. But unlike an interaction field, the connections between company and participant have been transactional, not interactional. The number of participants in the mobility interaction field of today is fluid and potentially unlimited; no one is untouched by it. But it is the automotive industry—covering the manufacture and ownership of cars, particularly ones that burn fossil fuel—which is, by necessity, experiencing a particularly critical moment. It is changing from an old-model, supply-chain industry to one that operates within a superfluid interaction field. As we'll see, Tesla, Waymo, and Uber, are leading examples in the evolution of all major participants, from traditional carmakers to interaction field companies, in mobility.

Frictions on the Roadways Are Easy to Identify

In the world of mobility, frictions are everywhere. If current rates of production and demand continue as they are, the number of automobiles worldwide will double between 2020 and 2050 to reach as many as 2.5 billion vehicles.[3] The number of automobiles on the planet is already producing significant frictions, particularly in the form of congestion within metropolitan areas—a serious productivity drain and health hazard. According to a 2018 report by transportation analytics firm INRIX, the yearly cost of congestion to every American was ninety-seven hours and $1,348, totaling $87 billion a year. Traffic congestion in the United Kingdom—a country with far fewer roadways, urban centers, cars, and people—cost some 8 billion pounds, or 1,317 pounds and 187 hours per driver.[4] These figures do not take into account the costs associated with the stress and frustration of coping (or failing to cope) with traffic.

The cost of mobility—of owning and operating an automobile, combined with all other transportation needs—is among the highest in any category of spending for the average American household, roughly $9,000 per year, including more than $2,000 for fuel.[5] According to the Union of Concerned Scientists (UCS), the burning of gasoline in cars and trucks accounts for close to one-fifth of US greenhouse-gas emissions. The broader transportation sector—which includes aircraft, railroads, and all forms of shipping—accounts for nearly 30 percent of emissions.[6]

Not only do these emissions pose serious risks to humanity in the long run, they also have hazardous effects on health in the short term. Passenger vehicles contribute significantly to the amount of particulate matter— molecules of nitrogen and carbon oxides—in our near atmosphere, which can increase the risk of contracting illnesses from bronchitis to cancer. Particulate matter, according to the UCS, is responsible for as many as thirty thousand deaths each year.[7]

Driving itself is also notoriously dangerous. According to the World Health Organization, there are 1.35 million road traffic deaths per year worldwide—an average of 3,700 per day. This is the leading cause of death among people ages five to twenty-nine. Young men seem particularly vulnerable: 73 percent of all road fatalities occur among males under the age of twenty-five. While the WHO notes that unsafe roads and unsafe vehicles contribute to deadly accidents, the most significant factors are human behaviors: speeding, driving under the influence, not wearing helmets (on motorcycles) or seatbelts, and distracted driving.[8]

These frictions have rubbed against one another, against car owners, and against society for years. The technologies exist to reduce and even eliminate them, and companies that have capitalized on the availability of these innovations have changed the old automotive industry into a superfluid mobility market, led by a few techno-pioneers.

Technologies That Solve Major Frictions

The challenge is to choose a technology that addresses these frictions now and is also flexible enough to evolve as new frictions appear over time and new technologies emerge and coalesce with existing solutions.

In the automotive sector, there are numerous technologies that impact many frictions, and each technology has its own timeline. Analysts typically identify four major technologies that could produce significant results: electrification, autonomous driving, sharing solutions, and connectivity. These technologies also enable new digital business models, such as subscription services. They can be defined and discussed in various ways and can include phenomena such as "connected driving experiences," "new models of ownership," and "seamless communications" with "smart ecosystems."[9] New or improved manufacturing methods and technologies are also likely to have significant effects on efficiency.

It is helpful to evaluate technologies in terms of the type of frictions they solve. These include consumer challenges, such as the high cost of ownership; industry challenges, such as the use of materials whose production has negative environmental impact (metals and plastics are the two major ones); and larger societal issues, such as CO_2 emissions or the reduction of accidents, which would save lives while also reducing healthcare costs.

A second dimension goes along a timeline. Some technologies have a shorter-term impact, while others only realize benefits over a longer time. An important aspect is the maturity of technologies. When Uber's former CEO Travis Kalanick first heard about Uber at a conference in France in 2008, the technology was relatively simple and newly available. With the company's cofounders, Kalanick was able to bring together the technologies that enabled the consumer to request a car by sending a text or pressing a button, identified the location of driver and passenger via GPS, and automatically charged the fare to the card on the user's account.

Another dimension is the extent to which the technology enables interactions across the nucleus, ecosystem, and market makers of the interaction field. Uber does not benefit from direct network effects but does benefit from indirect, or cross-side, effects. The more riders there are, the more drivers are attracted to Uber, but riders do not care how many other riders there are. So although there is a network effect for Uber, it is not a particularly strong one. Market makers are drawn to Uber for reasons other than ride hailing. For example, urban planners draw on Uber data to develop ways to ease traffic congestion.

The most successful companies in mobility have pursued initiatives in one or more of these technologies in order to build the interaction velocity that creates network effects, learning effects, and virality. Uber started with mobile as a core technology but entered the autonomous car business by purchasing Otto, a company started by a Google engineer. Waymo has launched a self-driving car and is also entering the ride-sharing market in direct competition with Uber and Lyft. Tesla started with electric cars as a core product but now focuses on the chip technology necessary for autonomous vehicles. It severed its relationship with chip producer Nvidia and produces its chips in-house. It also entered the ride-sharing market with the Tesla Network.

The Potential Impact of Solving the Frictions

Technology tends to be elusive and ephemeral. It proceeds down a windy road toward maturity. The "hype cycle" identified by research company Gartner, which describes the pattern that new technologies follow and how they evolve toward maturity and adoption, comes to mind: from the "peak of inflated expectations," to the "trough of disillusionment," then the "slope of enlightenment," and "plateau of productivity."[10] Often one technology must coalesce with another to have an impact in the market. It is a daunting task to monitor technologies, evaluate them, and predict their impact on solving major frictions. There are a number of influencing factors.

First is the likelihood that a company or the industry as a whole will adopt a certain technology. This factor is important in generating interaction velocity. Nobody does it alone. There are various degrees of adoption. Electrification of cars, for example, has wide industry adoption, while blockchain verification has a low adoption rate. It is beneficial when an industry or the major companies within it adopt a new technology.[11]

Second is the projected market demand in the near term versus the long term. Some technologies have broad market appeal and hence have large potential.[12] Lidar—light detection and ranging, short for light radar—for example, is the essential technology for self-driving cars. Hence, lidar has a very large market potential.

Third is the forecasted impact of solving the pain points of the consumer's everyday life around mobility or transportation, such as commuting, vacationing, and shopping. A challenge here is to define future life moments, perhaps identifying consumer scenarios ten years out, and to assess what impact new technologies will have on these episodes. Electric vehicles and advanced driver assistance are the most likely near-term technologies to have the greatest impact.

Evaluation of Participant Strategies in the Evolving Interaction Field

Next, we'll evaluate existing companies in terms of major strategies, such as:

- the types of data they collect;
- the technologies they have chosen;
- the character of their relationship with customers;
- the brand or value proposition; and
- the partnerships or collaborators in their ecosystem.

Given such factors, we can look at the key players in mobility—including Tesla, Uber, Waymo, and GM—to make better decisions about investments in various parts of the business (for example, charging stations versus different driving technologies), which will have an important impact on the development of an interaction field.

As of this writing, Waymo and GM have the edge over Tesla in autonomous driving. But Tesla has data gathered from more than a billion miles on real roads—all collected from its drivers—far more than Waymo has. Tesla could leverage this data to its advantage. Relative to the other major players, Tesla has placed different bets on achieving the various levels of autonomy. This will prove significant for the company in solving major frictions and staying ahead of the automotive incumbents.

In EVs, Tesla has the lead in so many respects: its technology (such as Hardware 3), its computer platform built on proprietary chips, its battery technology, its Supercharger network, and its retail outlets. It also has a significant advantage in over-the-air updates—software improvements delivered to the vehicle without the owner taking any action. As a result, Tesla's market valuation is much higher than that of GM or Ford.

Incumbents can't just follow the Silicon Valley technology companies. Industry analysts have defined four scenarios for how manufacturers such as BMW and Tesla will evolve by 2025.[13] If they fail to leverage the technologies they choose, or choose the wrong ones, they may stagnate or even become "fallen giants." If they succeed, they may evolve into a "hardware platform provider"—that is, a commodity carmaker with high volume but likely very little brand value. Or, they could evolve into a "data and mobility manager," focused on software and features, with far more interactions, and thus more potential for velocity, than the platform provider.

Another way to think of the role of the major participants in the interaction field is through the lens of new business models such as subscription services—currently a major focus for the automotive industry as more and more potential participants decide that they have no interest in owning a car. Essentially, these subscription programs provide access to vehicles for a fixed, all-inclusive monthly fee. Carmakers like Cadillac, Volvo, and Jaguar offer such services, as do start-up services such as Mobiliti and Fair. The programs are essentially a new form of traditional long-term rental or private leasing, but with two key differences: greater transparency and the flexibility to swap out vehicles during the course of the engagement.

Subscription models create new interaction fields, particularly for EVs, and there are three models that are likely to gain acceptance. The first is the one we know today: mobility solutions for a monthly fee. The next level is the bundling of services. Tesla, for example, currently bundles Supercharger access with the sale of its Model S. In the future, it could also bundle alternative transportation options like trains or scooters. It could combine with the Whim app, for example, which provides access to a whole ecosystem of services, including cleaning, refueling, battery charging, and battery leasing.[14]

There is another level of subscription that could further expand the superfluid mobility market. Subscription 3.0 might offer individually tailored and personalized packages of mobility, so it looks more like a membership than a subscription service. The service would employ machine learning to build a complete profile and predict the participants' car needs and overall transportation behavior, automatically adjusting the monthly membership. This would be the biggest interaction field opportunity because the power lies in the interaction—the platform is fed constantly with new data, and this data is used to hyper-personalize the service.

This is known as TAAS, transportation as a service, or MAAS, mobility as a service, and it has the potential to change everything. Interaction fields could deliver a level of convenience and personalization at a massive scale.

Which brand or company is most likely to succeed in this superfluid market? Nobody has that crystal ball. What is clear, though, is that companies like Tesla and Waymo have pulled the industry incumbents into a new era.

Tesla: An Energy Company

Yes, Tesla looks a lot like a carmaker in the traditional sense of the word. The company manufactures personal vehicles that are high performing and sleekly designed and that surpass industry safety standards. They also come equipped with autopilot features coordinated by high-tech sensors and cameras, which are connected to Tesla's cloud to receive over-the-air software updates. And, of course, the cars are powered by Tesla's electric engine, a proprietary technology that includes, significantly, the company's energy-storage systems.

I am willing to bet that more people know the name of Tesla's CEO than know that Tesla also sells solar panels, a Powerwall battery to store energy generated for domestic use, and the Powerpack, an industrial-scale energy-storage solution.

Tesla is not really a carmaker at all, but rather an energy company that sells cars. As such, Tesla has enormous potential to form an interaction field, one that intimately connects the energy sector with the mobility industry: solar-powered cars, trucks, buses, and trains, plugged in to solar-powered homes and buildings. Given its pioneering position in the sale of EVs, Tesla is in a better place than many other long-standing manufacturers to lead growth in the decades ahead.

As we've seen, there is little debate among leading consultancies and analysts investigating the automotive and mobility industries that the proliferation of EVs will be among the dominant revolutionary trends of the next thirty years.[15] It is, perhaps, a global imperative. The World Economic Forum views electrification as central to the "convergence of mobility and energy futures" and anticipates that battery electric vehicles (BEVs) will outnumber vehicles with a fuel-burning internal combustion engine (ICE) on roads before 2050.[16] The profitability of the two vehicles will see a similar switch, as ICE vehicles become less profitable beginning in the early 2020s and BEVs begin to see profit growth by 2030.[17] The market share of EVs is expected to grow from 6 percent in 2020 to 22 percent in 2030.[18] This will, of course, have significant effects for the oil and gas industries and the energy sector broadly, with oil demand expected to peak at one hundred million barrels per day in 2020.[19]

Tesla is addressing the friction that results from the mobility industry's reliance on unsustainable energy. This means Tesla has the potential to create an interaction field in the superfluid mobility market, by literally plugging into the energy sector. Because Tesla was born with this pursuit in mind, unlike traditional twentieth-century automotive manufacturers, it is uniquely situated for success. As industry boundaries continue to break down, Tesla is becoming the first interaction field company in the merged energy-mobility space. One can only expect that, as Tesla adds vehicles and charging stations to the roads, increasing their visibility and the virality of their offerings, the company's advantage will similarly increase.

From its beginning in 2003, Tesla has had a mission "to accelerate the world's transition to a sustainable energy future."[20] That is the kind of broad goal that defines an interaction field company—one with far-reaching benefits for society at large, well beyond the limits of any specific industry.

"Energy efficiency" is perhaps a good way to describe Tesla's budding super interaction field, and the extent to which it has reduced or eliminated frictions in the automotive industry. We can see it in the engine itself: whereas an ICE in a stereotypical car might be composed of as many as one thousand parts, Tesla's electric engine is built with as few as eighty. Engines with fewer parts tend to experience fewer maintenance issues and require fewer repairs.

If we look at the market from the consumer journey perspective, we see that friction can be both behavioral and physical. For environmentally aware drivers, every fill-up at the pump can produce a sense of guilt and shame, caused by an awareness that such behavior is deleterious to the environment and humankind's existence within it. Every trip to the service shop reminds consumers of their investment in hardware and the cost—in both time and money—that seems squandered on this mobility solution.

Pinpointing these two sources of friction allowed Tesla to hit the ground running in an era when people are hyperconscious of global climate change and its acceleration due to greenhouse gases, providing a base for a cross-industrial vision of Tesla's interaction field. Included within its network are the charging stations found at rest areas, strip malls, and other locations around the country, which are not only necessary for Tesla drivers but produce an added effect of visibility and virality. However, it is reasonable to assume that the majority of Tesla vehicles will be charged primarily and most often in their owners' garage or driveway, a fact that seamlessly merges Tesla's operation in the automotive sector with its products in the energy sector.

Tesla wants to power your car, through your home, using their batteries and solar panels, as part of its vision for being "the world's only vertically integrated energy company offering end-to-end clean energy products."[21] While Tesla's entry into the energy market—its solar roof tiles and batteries—has yet to gain consumer traction along the lines of its Model S or Model 3 vehicles, the ambition to do so illuminates the effectiveness of approaching a market with a view to reducing or eradicating existing frictions, such as where energy is wasted or spent counter to larger societal goals. Electrification of vehicles is now one of the defining characteristics of the evolving mobility industry, and debate as to whether Tesla will eventually succeed or fail as a business runs parallel to the debate about whether any other automotive manufacturer can match their success.

Waymo and the "New Way Forward in Mobility," or Uber "Über Alles"[22]

The car of the future is electric, yes, but it is also autonomous—that is, self-driving. Such machines are no longer a thing of the future; as of this writing, they are driving on the streets of several cities. With the introduction of self-driving and fully autonomous vehicles—those that require zero human operation to drive, maneuver, or park—the automotive-mobility industry is bound to go through a paradigm shift, remaining superfluid for the next several decades as interaction fields organize and emerge.

The possible scope of the change has been well imagined, and together with the emerging trends of cloud-connected and shared-use vehicles, electrification and automation will usher in a new era of transportation: one less dependent on personal ownership, asset investment, idle capacity, and waste, and more defined by mobility as an on-demand service.

Waymo is focusing on the frictions caused by car ownership. It is well known that personal vehicles spend the majority of their existence parked in a driveway or garage waiting to be used—as much as 95 percent of their lifetimes.[23] Uber seized that opportunity, providing a platform through which those cars could be put to use, not only to offer a valuable service for passengers but also for drivers. Potentially any person with a car, license, and insurance could now monetize an investment.

This enabled Uber to generate a $82.4 billion valuation at its IPO and radically upend the ride-hailing industry (in combination with similar services such as Lyft), threatening to put taxi services out of business. However, Uber has already found itself playing catch-up to a newer arrival on the scene, one whose service is strikingly more effective at reducing industry frictions: Waymo, whose name comes from "a new way forward in mobility."[24] The company started in 2009 as a spin-off of parent company Alphabet and was formerly known as Google's self-driving car project.

Waymo envisions a twenty-first-century automotive industry, in which vehicles are electric, autonomous, connected to the Internet of Things, and—crucially—shared. The basic service is not unlike Uber's: users download an app, set their location, input their destination, and hail a ride. But the car that arrives to chauffeur users from point A to point B is driverless, electric, and owned not by an individual but by Waymo. In this, Waymo exhibits the superfluidity of the automotive industry: the company recently announced plans to build a manufacturing facility in Michigan, but none of the cars produced there will be for sale to private individuals.[25]

When compared to a traditional auto manufacturer, the benefits of this shift in approach are immediately clear: Waymo controls its own supply and demand. A Waymo car, once produced, will never sit idly in a lot, unsold, but rather will be deployed into Waymo's interaction field. As part of Google's expansive, data-driven network, Waymo will theoretically determine the positioning of its mobility-service vehicles by identifiable frictions and opportunities within and between cities or regions where the market for Waymo already exists.

As with Tesla, Waymo's transformative effect is a consequence of its cross-industrial approach: it is a technology company that, to achieve its ambition of ushering in a "new way forward in mobility," has entered the car-manufacturing industry. Waymo differentiated itself from its competitors from the start, and it has forced the other industry transformers we've discussed—Tesla and Uber—to envision similar futures.

The vision of Tesla Network—in which Tesla owners can voluntarily rent out their vehicles while unused, similar to how Airbnb users rent out their apartments or homes—was conceived by Musk as early as 2016. This network depends on the autonomy of Tesla vehicles and regulatory approval, but Musk claimed at the time that such a service would reduce the cost of ownership to the point "where almost anyone could own a Tesla."[26] In 2018, Musk took the project a step further, announcing

Tesla's plans to operate its own fleet of shared-use, electric, and autonomous vehicles.

Musk believes Tesla is well positioned to outmuscle future competition, and there is reason to believe he's right. For starters, the Tesla Network model does not eliminate the possibility of personal vehicle ownership and so offers something Waymo does not, and will not, by simultaneously generating revenue through sales. Tesla's vehicle network is already far larger than Waymo's, with five hundred thousand vehicles and ten thousand Superchargers on the roads worldwide, as well as its flagship stores and showrooms where vehicles (as well as energy products) can be viewed, test-driven, and purchased.[27] Tesla's autonomous driving technology has already recorded more than one billion road miles across its vehicles, and its data collection and machine learning greatly outpace Waymo's analysis of its tens of millions of self-driven miles.

While Waymo faces a serious challenge to match Tesla's existent network, data collection, and technology (only Tesla vehicles receive over-the-air software updates), Uber's climb to maintain relevancy will be even steeper. Like Tesla and Waymo, Uber is in the process of developing a fleet of autonomous vehicles, with a mission to "bring safe, reliable self-driving transportation to everyone, everywhere."[28] To do so, Uber will have to eliminate drivers from its network and simultaneously negate its primary impact of engaging individuals' unused capacity. It is difficult to predict what the effects for the company will be.

The road will be even steeper for traditional car manufacturers and automotive suppliers, who will be forced to evolve and maneuver within a superfluid industry whose operating standards and business models will undergo irreversible shifts.

While some traditional automotive companies have adjusted their offerings to include subscription services and are pushing aggressively toward electrification, they do not capitalize on the superfluid market by envisioning future interaction fields within the larger mobility-services industry. Such modifications aim only to address frictions apparently smoothed by other industry actors, like Tesla and Waymo, who approach the industry with an interaction field perspective and thus more effectively harness opportunities to create efficiencies.

Conclusion: Interactions Are the Currency

In the vision of the Tesla Network and Waymo's autonomous taxi fleet, we see the future of mobility. Of course there will still be ownership, but mobility interactions will create new, shared, and exponential value for everyone. The anticipated effects of this change are staggering. According to the World Economic Forum, as much as $670 billion of industry value (and $3 trillion of societal value) is at stake by 2025.[29] With MAAS fleets utilizing autonomous and electric vehicles, transport will become four to ten times cheaper per mile than purchasing a new car.[30] The cost of financing vehicles is expected to drop 90 percent, of maintaining them 80 percent, of insuring them 90 percent, and of fueling them 70 percent.[31] Energy demand will be reduced by 80 percent and tailpipe emissions by 90 percent.[32] It has been estimated that the number of passenger vehicles on American roadways will drop from 247 million to 44 million. As fewer cars travel farther, reaching a lifetime potential of as many as one million miles, it is expected that 70 percent fewer passenger cars will be manufactured every year.[33] Taken together, these figures represent enormous opportunities for companies capable of developing strong interaction fields within the superfluid market, as well as for individual consumers who will pay less out of pocket for transportation and for a society less suffocated by congested roads and toxic fumes.

Such opportunity arises whenever a market becomes—or needs to become—superfluid to address frictions that grind against industry sectors or between an industry and society. Envisioning the interaction fields that could evolve requires a perspective broader than the industry itself, in order to encourage interactions and create synergies across previously disconnected channels. Whether observing the industry from an ecosystem (or, better, interaction field) perspective or through the lens of a consumer journey, identifying and seeking to reduce or eliminate frictions is the first step in building a super interaction field. Companies that do so effectively and expand their networks with velocity, such as Tesla, will be the ones poised to dominate the market once it reaches a solid and resta-bilized state—if it ever does.

Superfluid markets are, as we've seen, constantly evolving. They con-tinue to subsume new industries and categories, alter the structure of markets, change the nature of competition, and, in turn, contribute to the rise of customer expectations. It is the interaction velocity—not the technology itself—that powers the viral, network, and learning effects and enables the solving of frictions, pain points, strains, and inefficiencies that leads to significant improvements.

The same is true of business areas, such as fashion, that are also highly fluid, but are not so driven by technology and are instead more centered around consumer preferences. At Burberry, as we'll see in the next chap-ter, success in creating an interaction field has to do with decisions made at the intersection of business strategy, brand, and changing human behavior.

chapter nine

Delivering Customer Experiences

The Role of Brand and Business Strategy

For me, Burberry is a heartbreaking story. The company, more than 150 years old, was well on its way to establishing an interaction field with great velocity—and was already bringing huge change to the entire fashion industry—until Christopher Bailey, its brilliant and long-tenured chief creative officer, took on the additional role of CEO in 2014. Three years of declining sales followed. In 2017, a new CEO was appointed, and the shift led to a change in direction. But Bailey's work before becoming the CEO had been a pioneering effort that, I believe, could have resulted in a new model for a luxury fashion firm and could have solved some of the problems of the industry in general. Instead, the new management chose to follow a more traditional path, going more upscale in search of beefier margins and brand exclusivity.

It is a fascinating story nonetheless. Most importantly, it demonstrates that there is no industry or company that cannot be transformed into an interaction field enterprise—even one that does not seem to have a core technology as part of its product or service. Tractors, semifinished metal products, medicines, and cars—all of these things are solidly rooted in technology and are touched by AI, machine learning, and data analytics.

Fashion is ephemeral, emotional, and instinctive. But, in fact, Burberry did have a core technology, if a rather dated one.

That is what makes the story so intriguing and illuminating. Interaction fields are not about technology. They are not solely a phenomenon of social media. They are diverse networks of people and groups, all of whom participate in the development, distribution, and digestion of a product or service that they care about, can contribute to, and benefit from—and that they believe can bring good to the world beyond the product itself. Success in building an interaction field requires crafting a business strategy that aligns well with the DNA of the brand and the participants who engage most with the business. The Burberry story demonstrates how important it is for a business strategy to sync well with a company's brand, especially in today's crazy, volatile, and transient times.

Designed to Protect the British People

Burberry was founded in 1856 by Thomas Burberry, then a twenty-one-year-old cloth merchant, with the purpose of developing and selling outdoor clothing. The company said it was "founded on the principle that clothing should be designed to protect people from the British weather," and it was located in Basingstoke, a small city west of London.[1] Its clothing caught on, and Burberry opened a retail shop in London in 1891.

In 1888, Burberry patented a technology for waterproofing yarn that could be spun into a dense yet highly breathable and water resistant fabric known as gabardine. It was lighter than traditional fabrics, more waterproof, and more comfortable to wear. Soon enough, adventurers, explorers, and other rugged outdoor people were adopting and endorsing Burberry's gabardine clothing. During World War I, Burberry developed a new kind of outer garment especially for the military, which it initially called the Trench-Warm. It supplied the "services of three coats in one," according to Burberry's promotional material. First, there was the weatherproof, which could withstand hours of rain. Then a "light camel fleece short-warm," which could be worn under the third layer, a thick overcoat, when the weather turned especially nasty. The coat featured epaulets that could be used to secure a pair of gloves or a whistle, D rings from which to hang grenades, and a gun flap and a storm shield to protect small weapons from the rain. The coat was closed with big buttons, cinched with a broad belt, and had a high collar to keep the neck warm and dry. Used throughout the war by British infantrymen, it became known as the trench coat.

It was not until after the war that Burberry came out with the check-pattern cloth as a lining material for its raincoats. The pattern eventually became its signature look—today known as the Haymarket check.

After the war, Burberry kept on keeping on. Interesting to note that need to quickly get one's hands on a Burberry product was satisfied as early as 1934, when Burberry introduced same-day delivery within London, thanks to its dedicated transport van. From the 1970s to the 1990s, Burberry expanded dramatically. It extended its product range far beyond outerwear to include suits, shirts, pants, and accessories for children, women, and men. It licensed the Burberry name to independent producers and extended its reach by selling in shops around the world.

Just after the turn of the millennium, Burberry hit a rough patch, caused by a number of factors. With such a wide range of products available at so many locations, availability and duplication led to price cutting, always a peril for a luxury brand. Due to Burberry's popularity, it became a favorite of counterfeiters, who produced scarves and coats and sold them at drastically reduced prices. One industry observer called Burberry a very British basket case, one that was dangerously close to becoming the UK equivalent of Pierre Cardin, another fashion brand that overextended itself and, as a result, suffered a diminution of its cachet.[2] The Cardin name appeared on hundreds of licensed items, from cheap boxer shorts to pencil holders. Cardin himself became known as the "licensing king," and not in a good way.

Then, starting around 2002, things got worse. A number of less-than-stellar cultural icons became enamored of the Burberry brand and flaunted it in very public ways. Some accounts credit (or blame) Danniella Westbrook, an actress on the popular English TV soap opera *EastEnders*, with dragging down the brand image. She played Samantha Mitchell, a teenager in a family living in the working-class London neighborhood. She was much in the news during her tenure on the show, which lasted off and on from 1990 to 2016. Westbrook's cocaine addiction and two marriages got a lot of media attention. She went into rehab in 2002, came out, and did a too-revealing TV interview that made it clear that the rehab had not been particularly successful. It was during that time that Westbrook famously stepped out swathed all in Burberry. She wore a Burberry check miniskirt and carried a Burberry check shoulder bag. Her young daughter wore a Burberry kilt and a second child was tucked into a pram lined and adorned with still more Burberry tartan.

Soon enough, Burberry clothing and the unmistakable check pattern became associated with what is known in England as "chav" culture. The origin of the term is obscure, but its meaning is clear. As the *Oxford English Dictionary* describes, a chav is "a young person of a type characterized by brash and loutish behavior and the wearing of designer-style clothes (esp. sportswear); usually with connotations of a low social status." Chav culture is also tied to football hooliganism, and Burberry garments became so associated with rowdy game-day behavior that they were banned at some venues.

Not what the marketers ordered. Burberry found itself in a tough position. The degraded brand image that resulted from the strange association with chav culture and hooliganism was hardly the company's only problem. It did not have much leverage with consumers for two reasons. First, it sold largely through retailers, and thus had little control over how its products were displayed, presented, and sold. Second, the signature product, the trench coat, was both expensive and long-lasting—by design unaffected by seasonal fashion trends—so the people who truly valued the brand had only infrequent contact with it.

The company had also weakened and overextended itself in the rush for growth, so the economics were not good and profitability was low. The company was seen as a traditional British manufacturer, not known for innovation or consumer responsiveness.

Given all this, Burberry might have taken a standard path toward refreshing and rebuilding the brand. It could have closed stores, cut costs, shrunk the line, come out with new advertising and marketing approaches. Instead, beginning around 2006, Burberry began to transition from value-chain thinking and moved toward the development of an interaction field.

Burberry Builds a Platform

Burberry started with a platform model by building the nucleus. Despite the missteps with chav culture, Burberry did have an understanding of the fashion goals of the people it saw as core participants: They have a rather traditional British sensibility. They don't aspire to own a famous brand and don't hop on trends. Although the Haymarket check is instantly recognizable to all those in the know, the true believers are not ones for conspicuous logo display. Nor is their goal in purchasing a raincoat really to keep dry and warm, since there are a thousand and one forms of outerwear available that will help solve the challenges of rain and cold. What the Burberry nucleus participants care most about is British culture: the land, history, language, literature, musicians, actors, celebrities, theater, bands, art, and fashion.

But here's an interesting feature of Burberry participants. They do not really have much interest in shopping. They don't particularly want to interact with British culture in shops, stores, or especially malls. An occasional stop at Burberry's flagship store on Regent Street in London would probably be enough for them. There they can select from the full range of Burberry coats, scarves, shoes, belts, ponchos, capes, sweaters, jewelry, blouses, and skirts. They can also get their purchases tailored and monogrammed. And they can stop in for a meal at Thomas's, where they can enjoy British classic cuisine with ingredients sourced from small farms and artisan suppliers.

But that's London, a special occasion, and the store is as full of gawkers and tourists as it is of true believers. Yes, there are some five hundred Burberry-branded outlets around the world, but that's a small number compared to some premium brands such as Gucci, Armani, or Ralph Lauren.

Burberry realized that it could build a nucleus of participants who actually preferred online interactions by creating a platform where they could browse, shop, and buy. Importantly, it would be a venue that enabled them to interact—when and how they chose—with other people who valued British style and enduring fashion.

Burberry created Burberry.com, an unusual move for a global fashion company at the time. Many luxury brands in particular were reluctant to go online because they worried that it would somehow cheapen their image. Burberry was the first company of its kind to build a digital infrastructure that enabled all nucleus participants—consumers, employees, investors, suppliers, headquarters staff, back-office people, warehouse operators, and retailers—to connect. Burberry became the first fully integrated and fully digital social enterprise in the fashion industry.

To build the number of customer participants in the nucleus with high interaction velocity, Burberry focused sharply on millennials who were interested in global society and cultures. This consumer contrasted with those of Burberry's competitors, who targeted well-to-do ladies who lunch and other baby boomers.[3] The company found that many millennials, who did not care much for trench coats, did care a great deal about British culture and that fashion was one way for them to express that passion.

My daughter Sara is a good example of the participant Burberry is after. She would never be found in a Burberry store—no time, no interest. She would never dress herself from head to toe in the Haymarket check. (I'm not sure she even knows that name.) But she does love British culture. She is drawn to events and experiences around it, and the Burberry approach has attracted her. She follows Burberry fashion as she once followed the British band One Direction. She opines on Burberry's products, shares news about recent releases, and discusses purchases her friends have made. There are millions of people like Sara out there, who want to interact with a slice of Britishness. Even if Sara only purchases a few, if any, Burberry items, she must be seen as a nucleus participant who helped Burberry achieve interaction dominance in its field.

The Burberry platform also made it easy for participants from around the world to join in the fun, even in locations far removed from any outlet where Burberry goods are sold. Although its physical expansion had caused problems, Burberry learned that the love of British style is hardly confined to Brits and Americans; rather, it extends to consumers around the world. China, in particular, is home to some of Burberry's most passionate participants.

That is why, as Burberry began to build a network of market makers, it reached out to a number of Chinese fashion bloggers, including Gogoboi, Li Beika, Mr. Bags, and Dipsy. Gogoboi does not fit the image of the traditional British Burberry buyer, nor does he push the brand toward a global interpretation of chav. Born in 1983, his real name is Ye Si, and he has become an important influencer in the Chinese fashion world. He studied English at university, has a background in fashion journalism, and became widely known for his distinctive "snarky" style—"ridiculing celebrities and cultural icons alike." But his penchant for ridicule has not prevented Gogoboi from taking advantage of his own online celebrity—or *wanghong*, as it is known in China—to make a buck. He created a store on WeChat that showcases a range of high-end goods and established an agency called Missionary to represent and mentor social media personalities.[4]

Although buoyed by its success in building its platform and field, Burberry did not abandon its physical assets. In fact, the company saw that it could turn its relative physical scarcity into a benefit by leveraging the flagship store as a digital presence.

To that end, the Regent Street store was completely reinvented and reopened in 2013 to provide interactive experiences for its participants, both in-store and online. It featured a digitally enabled gallery space to display clothing and accessories, huge screens, and satellite technology to enable livestreaming of in-store events.

Given the global interest, Burberry rethought its runway shows. These line introductions had traditionally been organized as exclusive insider events; that was what made them glamorous and appealing. Burberry made a radical departure and opened up their shows to the general public around the world. Using video technology from Sky television, Burberry could broadcast fashion shows—not only from the London location, but also from stores in Paris, New York, and Milan—to the laptops and mobile devices of consumers around the world, so that everyone could view and opine on the latest collections in real time. In-store, sales associates could connect with participants and check their product preferences and purchase history using the Burberry app on their iPads.

Online videos featuring Burberry fashions were made "shoppable." Consumers could choose items with a click, which allowed Burberry to learn what merchandise was most preferred by consumers, just as Netflix learns about its viewers' preferences. Burberry deducted the price of the merchandise from a credit card and delivered it within weeks to a shopper's home or to one of Burberry's seven hundred stores. Burberry became, in effect, a direct-to-consumer company like Warby Parker, long before that idea really took off.

This capability also meant that customers were financing the production of Burberry's collections, because they were only produced after a sale was made. It was essentially a bespoke service with a just-in-time, lean inventory process that reduced both cost and waste.

Burberry was on the way to perfecting a new business model for the fashion industry, one that reversed the order of the traditional value chain and that many other fashion retailers would pick up and adapt for their own use. In the first cycle of development, a product was designed in close interaction with consumers and a limited quantity was produced. Then the globally broadcast fashion shows determined market demand and sold the products.

This led to a second cycle of manufacturing, delivery, and distribution. Building scale followed in close alignment with the actual order book. In 2016, Burberry further innovated around this new operating model by launching the "see now, buy now" show at London Fashion Week, considered by many fashion industry experts as the opening of a new era and held up as a solution to long-standing problems of the industry.[5] But while Burberry pioneered the model from 2014 to 2016—and had an enormous advantage because of its large number of direct connections with consumers—the major industry players eventually caught on. Tommy Hilfiger launched the TommyNow line in 2018, where Facebook Live was made shoppable and items could be purchased via Pinterest, Instagram, and Snapchat.[6]

What are the fashion industry's chronic problems? Sustainability tops the list. The industry's water consumption is growing. Its carbon footprint is expanding. It creates huge amounts of waste. According to the US Environmental Protection Agency, almost thirteen metric tons of clothing wind up in landfills each year. Global textile production emits 1.2 billion tons of greenhouse gases annually (more than international flights and maritime shipping combined). The fashion industry is responsible for up to 10 percent of global CO_2 emissions, 20 percent of the world's industrial wastewater, 24 percent of insecticides, and 11 percent of pesticides, according to some estimates.[7]

Powerful industry advocates seek solutions to these problems, in part because they really matter to one significant participant: the consumer. Younger consumers simply have more common sense for social and environmental issues. They also value immediacy; they seek to purchase exactly the products they discover, without delay.[8] They say, "If I can get a product within an hour and a half with my Amazon Prime membership, why do I have to wait months to purchase something in the store?" Burberry took all the right steps toward building out this new business and operating model. It was leading the industry.

A key to Burberry's success was its direct connection with consumers and relatively high interaction rate through social channels and its own digital platform. Burberry reached out to market makers, including celebrities not directly connected to the brand and even competitors. The number of interactions rapidly increased, such that the Chinese bloggers collectively have more daily Twitter followers than America's tweeter in chief, President Trump, does. Of Burberry's Chinese participants, 91 percent engage, shop, and buy on mobile phones via Weibo or WeChat, apps that collectively reach over 1.5 billion consumers in China alone.

In general, Burberry generated more interactions than any other fashion brand, even more than mainstream, iconic brands such as Ralph

Lauren. By 2014, it was leading every fashion and luxury brand in terms of direct interactions with consumers, as measured by Facebook, Instagram, Twitter, and YouTube. It had over thirty-two million followers, versus Ralph Lauren's fifteen million and Hugo Boss's ten million. Sales growth outperformed the entire luxury market. Financial performance and stock-price performance followed.

Burberry became the leading digital and social enterprise in the fashion industry, which attracted many consumers and fans but also competitors, who quickly copied the Burberry innovations.

Unfortunately, Burberry could not keep the velocity going enough to create a virtuous cycle. Around 2014, the major luxury fashion houses—including LVMH, with Louis Vuitton, and Kering, with Gucci—started to pursue direct social interactions with consumers, largely using Instagram. Gradually, the Burberry advantages disappeared as other brands built larger nuclei. Gucci is an outstanding example, because it hit the sweet spot between creativity and technology or, put another way, between art and science. Alessandro Michele, the creative director, delivered on the aesthetic preferences of millennials, while the site creators doubled down on technology and social media. By 2019, Burberry had about 14.6 million followers on Instagram, while Louis Vuitton had 34.2 million and Gucci had 32.2 million. Hugo Boss and Ralph Lauren had equaled Burberry.

While growth in the number of nucleus participants does not necessarily indicate the velocity of each company, it is indicative of how Burberry squandered its leadership position. There are a number of reasons for this decline. Most important, there was a change in leadership. The CEO, Angela Ahrendts, left to join Apple, and the board of directors made the fateful decision to hand the CEO responsibilities to Christopher Bailey, the chief creative officer. He did not have the operational experience or commitment to further the interaction field model while the industry faced a cyclical retail slowdown. Burberry experienced flat or declining sales over several years. Bailey was soon replaced by a new CEO who had made his mark at Celine, a fashion house owned by the upscale LVMH conglomerate. The new CEO brought experience in turnarounds of fashion houses built on the traditional value-chain model.

The CEO decided to push Burberry in the opposite direction. Instead of making luxury more accessible to young global audiences, he took it further upscale, which did not fit the interaction field approach and its direct connection to millennials. This shows the critical importance of leadership and vision in creating interaction field companies.

As of this writing, the fashion industry has evolved, and many other companies have adopted some or all of Burberry's successful practices and are building out their own interaction fields. Burberry still considers itself one of the leading companies in reaching digital and social participants globally, but the turnover in leadership has caused major changes to the company's fortunes. Burberry is now at the beginning of a five-year turnaround and repositioning effort. These developments only go to show that an interaction field does not operate on autopilot. It needs constant attention from the company at its center.

The heartbreaking part of the story (for me, anyway) is that Burberry had all the makings of a game-changing interaction field. It could have continued to influence the way the fashion industry operates and redefined the category. Burberry had many different options. One was to build an interaction field for all things British. As it brought in more ecosystem and market participants, it could have created its own marketplace, with a range of high-end offerings for the global millennial consumer—products and services that, like Burberry, seem to embody the lifestyle, attitude, culture, and luxury of the British. Another interaction field option was to stay true to its accessible luxury position in the fashion industry and focus on building a range of new business models that would make Burberry even more accessible. These might have included subscription services or sharing and other new ownership models. Burberry also could have combined its interaction field with others, such as Alibaba's Tmall or Chinese retailer JD.com's luxury e-commerce platform Toplife, now owned by Farfetch.

Instead, the business and financial challenges—exacerbated by the lack of visionary leadership—led Burberry to retreat and focus on optimizing the traditional value-chain model. As it reconfigured—refocusing product, marketing, and distribution—competing labels zoomed ahead, and Burberry now finds itself in the midst of another turnaround. Today, of the twenty top fashion companies as measured by sales volume, Burberry comes in at the bottom of the list.[9]

Going upscale might prove to be the right strategy for Burberry. For the fiscal year 2018, profits were up slightly, but sales were flat and the company will continue to face strong headwinds from French and Italian luxury labels. LVMH and Kering are among the fastest-growing businesses in the luxury sector and have significant resources to fund new ventures. LVMH delivers more than five times the economic profit that Burberry does, and Kering delivers as much as three times.

There are lessons to be learned from the Burberry story. First, and perhaps most important, is that building a powerful interaction field is not a matter of technology. Technology does not drive velocity. Technology, ultimately, can be copied. It is the business strategy and brand strategy enabled by technology that deliver a different customer experience, which creates a sustainable competitive advantage.

Nor is it a matter of what industry you're in. Fashion, semifinished metal products, action cameras—it doesn't matter. It can become an interaction field enterprise. Yes, it requires technology and a platform and all of that. But what it really takes is vision. Burberry had it, then lost it.

Strategy Powered by Enabling Technology

What truly matters is to figure out a way to define a business strategy, brand strategy, and customer experience—given an enabling technology infrastructure—and align these pieces in a way that sets up the conditions for an interaction field to develop, grow, and build velocity. Let's take a look at each of those components.

Business strategy, as traditionally defined by such theorists as Michael Porter, is about where and how to compete, as well as what *not* to do and where *not* to compete. Burberry's strategy was to evolve from a manufacturer of trench coats to a global fashion retailer, with a vision of becoming the first fully digital luxury company. To do that, it would compete through an enabling technology. Digital, social, and technological innovation would be at the center of its business and would change the way the company engaged with consumers. The strategy was to be interactional rather than transactional. The goal was not just to make a sale, or even to convert the shopper to Burberry, but rather to create a direct relationship with the consumer through frequent, meaningful interactions that could extend into realms beyond fashion and apparel.

The decision of where to compete was unusual for a luxury brand and represented a major strategic direction. Burberry, like other luxury firms, had traditionally targeted older consumers who had significant discretionary incomes and preferences for luxury lifestyles. But Burberry made the decision to target millennials around the world. These younger consumers are more fashion forward and trendsetting, and these characteristics helped refresh the Burberry brand. Millennial consumers are also digitally and socially savvy, which fit Burberry's vision. Angela Ahrendts, Burberry's CEO until 2014, said, "I grew up in a physical world, and I speak English. The next generation is growing up in a digital world, and they speak social."

Millennials have high expectations for what a brand should be able to deliver in terms of convenience, quality, values orientation, newness, and price. They demand more personalization and want instant gratification. Burberry was able to meet these expectations through its new business model and digital innovations, including the "see now, buy now" effort.

The younger generation also has high expectations for brands. They consider the company's practices and mission in light of their own values. Here, Burberry had an advantage as an authentic, heritage brand, British through and through. Burberry, after all, had supplied the garments for Ernest Shackleton's extraordinary South Pole expedition at the beginning of the twentieth century.

Burberry decided to celebrate Britishness—in art, entertainment, culture, music, sports, and more—which, by association, made the brand even more attractive to a large global audience and created enormous potential for interaction velocity. This focus increased the frequency and quality of interactions between Burberry and its participants, beyond buying luxury products.

The business and brand strategies translated into a differentiating customer experience for younger audiences. Millennials had come to disdain the fashion industry for its relentless focus on the new and its habit of discarding the out of date willy-nilly. Millennials not only hated the waste, they also were trending away from ownership altogether, embracing rental, reuse, and sharing services.

So, given the direct relationship that Burberry had developed with its participants, it was in a position to create a consignment site such as the RealReal. Or it might have adapted the subscription-rental model, which was pioneered by New York–based Rent the Runway in 2009, followed by Le Tote in San Francisco and YCloset in China. These services give participants access to a range of clothing and accessories they could never afford to buy. Rent the Runway says that it gives participants "fashion freedom," because you can try endless items without having to commit to any of them. If something doesn't work out, you don't have to worry about returning it or disposing of it. It's going back anyway. Rent the Runway takes care of cleaning and repair, so you don't have to worry about dry-cleaning expenses or inefficient use of water or cleaning products. Rent the Runway offers two different plans, starting at $69 per month. Pretty cheap for a constantly refreshed wardrobe.

YCloset participants are mostly young women, age eighteen to thirty-five, who care about fashion but also have to dress practically for work. A subscriber can make unlimited rentals, but the typical participant rents about twelve different outfits monthly. YCloset met some resistance at first, largely because people had their doubts about wearing clothing that some other, unknown person had already worn, but the company has addressed that issue. It overcame consumer concerns about hygiene and cleaning by opening up its own dry-cleaning facilities and providing washing and maintenance services through partners.

Burberry might also have offered a subscription service like Stitch Fix or Trunk Club. With these, subscribers receive a monthly assortment of clothing. At the end of the period, they can purchase the garments or return them. Such a service would have given Burberry enormously valuable information about the preferences of its participants.

Burberry could easily have expanded its offerings, just as Amazon evolved from a traditional retailer to become a third-party marketplace.

Burberry might have built a marketplace of synergistic, start-up brands, and thus brought in many more participants to the nucleus. This is successfully being done by businesses such as Reformation, I.AM.GIA, Supreme, and Everlane. These start-up brands seek to disrupt the traditional businesses in fashion. By building a marketplace for a range of brands and products, Burberry could have built its interaction field and increased velocity.

One of the key decisions you must make when building an interaction field is whether to build your own platform or to participate in an existing one created by a partner or even a competitor. Burberry, in effect, did both. It created Burberry.com and then extended its reach by participating in others. These included Toplife, a platform that features luxury goods and a premium delivery service called JD Luxury Express, and Tmall, which launched the Luxury Pavilion for brands such as Burberry, Hugo Boss, and Maserati, complemented with livestreamed fashion shows.[10]

It made sense for Burberry to participate in these platforms to extend its reach, because it had already established itself as an interaction field on Burberry.com. Burberry was able to benefit from being an ecosystem participant in other fields, while retaining control of its brand and its customer data, and the insights gained from that information.[11]

It is an enormous challenge for the fashion industry to deliver on ever rising and changing customer expectations. Customers not only want convenience, quality, and price, they also want speed, variety, flexibility, and transparency. But fashion has long been about the opposite of all those things. Burberry had the chance to solve some of those problems by reducing the lag time between discovery and purchase. It might have used its online presence to create a steady stream of inspiration and options—with new offerings daily—so that participants did not have to wait for elaborate fashion shows and coordinated collections. Just give me new stuff now, but don't make it until I ask for it.

Burberry didn't go that big or bold, but there are glimmers of hope. In the fall of 2018, Burberry seemed to be back on its earlier track. The new chief creative officer, Riccardo Tisci, came on board in March 2018 and things started to speed up. Burberry offered a Thomas Burberry mono-gram T-shirt, available through WeChat and Instagram for twenty-four hours only. This method of launching a new collection is known in the industry as a drop, and it has become very popular because it creates a sense of urgency and the illusion of scarcity. Tisci also made sure that his debut collection would be available almost instantly—just thirty min-utes after being showcased at London Fashion Week.[12] Then, Burberry announced it would follow a new release rhythm: new products would be introduced on the seventeenth of every month. According to Tisci, one of the most important aspects of the initiative is to keep up constant communication with the company's nucleus participants. Burberry may yet push the fashion industry out of its old model and into the age of the interaction field.

The Burberry story is also instructive because it highlights the critical role of leadership in creating and sustaining an interaction field company. It shows how the organization must often be reinvented to achieve veloc-ity, as I'll discuss in next chapter.

chapter ten

Velocity Versus Clicks

On Becoming an Interaction Field Company

I'm hoping that by now you have become intrigued enough by the concept of the interaction field that you are entertaining the thought that it might be a good model for your company. The next question is quite obvious: Exactly how do you move in that direction, especially if you are a traditional pipeline company, a large legacy enterprise, or a start-up with a relatively conventional model? (That's almost everybody!)

In this chapter, I will do my best to give some practical guidance. The best way to do that is to analyze the initiatives of two more successful interaction field companies, Mars Petcare and Haier appliances, and then generalize from their experiences, while reviewing some of the other companies we have discussed along the way.

Realize the Interaction Field: Mars Petcare

Let me start by saying this: the foundation for an interaction field already exists. In a world where everything connects, the basis is there because nothing operates in isolation. For most businesses, it will only be necessary to discover the interaction field in which the company already functions, and then to expand its presence therein. The interaction field may include the entirety of your organization or discrete operations within it, and the challenge to your business could be deciding which interaction field is most advantageous to pursue.

Take Mars, Incorporated. Mars is known worldwide for its ubiquitous candies—M&M's, Snickers, Twix (all billion-dollar brands)—but its largest business is, in fact, Mars Petcare. It owns over fifty businesses and several billion-dollar brands, including Pedigree, Royal Canin, and Whiskas.[1] While Mars has been selling pet foods since the 1930s, starting with the purchase of Chappie in the United Kingdom, the company has, in the last few years, transitioned from a standard supply-chain manufacturer and distributor of consumer packaged goods (CPGs) to a leader in the pet-care industry. It achieved this by building the foundations of an interaction field company. As of this writing, Mars Petcare is in a $75 billion-per-year market that is expected to grow to $95 billion by 2021.[2]

The CPG business is famously stagnant. It is based on traditional supply-chain economics and asset-heavy business models. Product innovation, customization, and differentiation can only carry a business so far, and the industry ultimately provides little room for growth. It is easy—far too easy—for companies in this model to focus on what they see as their end product.

Let's say that product is a bag of dog food. There are many variations: It can be made with fish, turkey, chicken, beef, lamb, grains, and vegetables. It can be packaged in a five-pound bag, a ten-pound bag, or a fifteen-pound bag. Ingredients can be added or subtracted to deliver different benefits—to help control weight, strengthen bones, or add sheen to the coat. A bag of dog food, therefore, is not much different from a bag of M&M's: original, peanut, peanut butter, pretzel, almond, crispy, caramel, fun size, king size, party size—the list goes on and on.

What happens when a customer buys a bag of M&M's? If they're anything like me, they eat them. Right away. Sometimes I will save some for later. Maybe I will share them with my wife. But that is about all the benefit I get from the M&M's—and, importantly, that's all that I, the consumer, intended to get. I did not want much more from my M&M's than a few moments of satisfaction.

Here is where the difference between M&M's and dog food comes in. When a customer buys a bag of pet food, that interaction—the purchase of a product—takes place in a much more complex field of engagement. The customer is, presumably, a pet owner. The purchase of pet food is one interaction within a complex array of interactions the pet owner will have. She will likely engage with a breeder or an adoption center, with veterinarians and animal hospitals, and with specialized retailers and professionals that provide all kinds of products (toys, collars, leashes) and services (training, nutrition) to pets and pet owners alike.

You can imagine the various activities that a pet owner engages in on a regular basis—feeding, walking, monitoring health—each with a number of specific actions designed to achieve certain goals. Actions required to monitor health, for example, might involve finding a specialist veterinarian, scheduling appointments, or taking the pet to physical therapy sessions.

So the pain points, problems, challenges, and strains of pet ownership clearly extend far beyond buying food. But food is where Mars Petcare and Nestlé Purina, the two largest companies in the industry, have focused their product and brand portfolios. Their goal was to push pet food onto retail shelves, instead of addressing the real challenges and needs of pets and their owners. It is not surprising, therefore, that the pet food industry has been stagnant for years.

It is simple, and perhaps obvious, to say, but for a company to transition from a traditional supply chain or run-of-the-mill platform to a full-fledged interaction field company, the opportunities for creating an interaction field must first be discovered and clearly defined. And that is what Mars Petcare finally did.

Between 2016 and 2018, Mars Petcare—a company with $17 billion in annual revenue—spent roughly $14 billion on acquisitions and initiatives to develop the pet-care interaction field. Its mission: to create "a better world for pets." The largest acquisitions were those that put Mars Petcare directly in touch with its customers. In 2017, it acquired VCA, a chain of animal hospitals with eight hundred locations. In 2018, it acquired Linnaeus Group and AniCura—veterinarian hospital chains in

the United Kingdom and Europe, respectively. According to Leonid Sudakov, a president at Mars Petcare, the company became the world's largest employer of veterinarians, treating over ten million pets a year.[3]

In 2016, Mars Petcare also established a Connected Solutions divi-
sion, a concentrated effort to create and develop the pet-care interaction
field. Connected Solutions was established with two priorities: to connect
with its customers (both pets and pet owners) and to solve pain points in
their lives.

At the core of Mars Petcare are the interactions between its eighty-
five thousand Petcare associates and four hundred million pets around the
world (there is a total of about one billion). In the United States, pets are
full-fledged members of some eighty-five million households, or about 68
percent of the total.[4]

The goal is to improve pet health through nutrition and veterinary
care. To do that, Lung Huang, the Head of Growth Solutions at Kinship,
Mars Petcare, says the key is to amass proprietary, "first-party data" from
participants.[5] This, he says, is the "new currency of success."

This strategy was essential to establishing more direct relationships
between Mars and customers and professionals within the pet-care industry, through which the company became more familiar with the specific
needs, frictions, and efficiencies within the industry, and thus became
further equipped to facilitate, spawn, and enhance interactions therein.
By increasing the volume and velocity of the interactions within this field,
the company gained clearer insight into where it could direct its resources
to continually advance its goal of creating a better world for pets.

Here is not, perhaps, the place to detail the extent of Mars Petcare's
interaction field, as it follows similar examples we've discussed thus far.
Like other interaction field companies, Mars Petcare developed a nucleus, identified an ecosystem and market makers, formed strategic partnerships and collaborations, and created a platform where these various
members can solve problems and innovate with one another directly.
What Mars Petcare demonstrates is that, even in an industry where
there is a well-optimized global supply chain that efficiently churns out
products to be delivered to the retailer's shelf, there are opportunities

to create an interaction field that will deliver shared business value for participants.

Connected Solutions evolved into a comprehensive platform called Kinship, which Sudakov refers to as a "coalition for the pet industry."[6] It is precisely the kind of interaction field platform we have been discussing: one that brings together customers, collaborators, and competitors to solve problems within the pet-care industry. Kinship connects "a ton of different types of solutions that today seem disjointed, and don't really feed into one another, into something that can be a real support system" for pet owners.[7]

While providing a one-stop source of information and services for pet owners, Kinship also exposes Mars Petcare to promising start-ups and innovations within the industry that the company can engage with as a partner or investor. One initiative, the Companion Fund, has led to investments in as many as twenty start-ups that deal with nutrition, care, and technology to transform the experience for pet parents. Mars Petcare offers a Fitbit-like device for pets called Whistle and, using its massive data trove, can do genetic analysis of your pet's ancestry.

Kinship also brings many ecosystem participants into the interaction field. For example, it provides remote health-care consultations to pet owners in Russia, where there is an enormous unmet demand for these services. Kinship also provides a mobile medical care service, which arranges for pet care to come to you. Eventually, these pet home health-care services could include nursing assistance and rehabilitation care, physical therapy, disease management, and more.

As we have seen time and again with interaction field companies, the mind-set behind Mars Petcare and Kinship looks to the growth of the entire field, not just of Mars Petcare, as a measure of its achievement. "It's not just about us being successful by ourselves," says Sudakov. It's also about "us being successful because we will be at the fulcrum of the bigger coalition for the industry and its future."[8]

Mars Petcare has built out its interaction field and is on the way to delivering on its mission of creating a better world for pets and pet owners. With this example, I hope to make the point that whatever it is your company creates—steel bars, tractor trailers, high-performance cameras, or dog food—it cannot be seen as the finished product. The end result of production and manufacture is merely the foundation for the interaction field. The interaction field company does not think about what their product is, but why it is.

Consider MercadoLibre, which manages Latin America's biggest online marketplace, similar to Amazon and Alibaba. Chief Marketing Officer Sean Summers told me that one of the company's major goals is to shorten response time. Currently MercadoLibre delivers to 80 percent of consumers in Argentina, Brazil, and Mexico within forty-eight hours. The target is twenty-four hours. MercadoLibre also operates Mercado Pago, a financial services technology firm. According to Summers, 58 percent of Argentineans are not part of the banking system. They use cash to buy products and pay bills. "We want to enable them to be part of the financial system," Summers said, "so we can essentially eliminate cash."

Summers thinks like an executive from an interaction field company. He does not talk about the product, but rather about what the product can do for consumers' lives. He focuses on the frictions that exist in the interactions between consumers and MercadoLibre. Forty-eight-hour delivery? Using cash? Both are frictions that can be reduced or eliminated.

Take Klöckner & Co. The company's ability to transition to an interaction field started with its realization that the supply and sale of steel was inefficient and antiquated. The industry suffered from problems such as long waits for delivery, incorrect order fulfillment, and high inventory levels. Klöckner set out to streamline the process to eradicate these problems for itself and the industry. Tesla, to use another example, sells cars, but it is not a car company per se; it is an energy company that sells cars, photovoltaic panels, and energy storage solutions. Even GoPro can be seen in a similar way: its product is synonymous with a certain lifestyle, characterized by the high-octane thrills of extreme sports. GoPro is an adventure company that sells cameras.

Interaction field companies accomplish what no other corporate form or business model has accomplished so far. They get very close to customers. They truly become a part of their lives, integrate into their activities, and earn the permission to solve major and minor challenges, problems, frictions, and pain points.

To do all this, companies considering making a transition to the interaction field model ask themselves fundamental questions:

- Why does our company or product exist?
- What problems do we—or can we—help solve?
- Who will collaborate with us to solve these problems?
- How are we integrating seamlessly into the lives of our customers?

The answers to these questions will open your eyes to latent interaction fields. And the answer always rests at the consumer's doorstep. To become an interaction field company, you must shoulder the burdens of the entire interaction field you wish to be a part of.

While the first step in the process is often no more than a reorientation of thinking to the interaction field perspective, it is, in some cases, necessary to go further and reorganize the business itself. As Leonid Sudakov says, one of Mars Petcare's primary lessons from their transformation was that "nothing kills the signals between customers" and your business more than "layers of bureaucracy in your organization."[9]

Stripping away these layers is no small task, but it can be done, and the potential for creating a potent interaction field can be seen clearly in the example of Haier appliances.

Structure for Velocity: Haier Appliances

Haier, a global manufacturing company founded in China in 1984, is the world's largest supplier of "white goods"—those familiar home appliances such as washing machines, fridges, and freezers—as well as air conditioners, microwave ovens, TVs, and water heaters. For years, Haier's business model was classic. The company produced a limited portfolio of products in standard configurations to avoid too much complexity. It achieved high value with minimal defects, high productivity, and low waste. It optimized internal resources. To keep a tight rein on production and distribution, Haier built up a rigid hierarchical organization with a fat middle-management layer. A boom in China's middle class in the 1980s created a market highly receptive to Haier's offerings, and demand for Haier products and the company's conservative approach enabled it to grow quickly without major hiccups, build an admirable reputation worldwide, and achieve profitability.

But in the last two or three decades, the competition has grown from Chinese and Korean brands, as well as Japanese, European, and American competitors. Appliances have become largely a commodity business: dull and utilitarian when compared to smart devices and digital products. Haier, with all the characteristics, assets, and liabilities of a conventional value-chain company, was in jeopardy of slowing growth, dwindling share, and relegation to the world of low-margin manufacturers like General Motors, General Electric, and any other entity with the word "general" in its name.

Appliance manufacturers are typically hierarchical, large, and benefit from economies of scale. The more they increase production volume, the more they can drive down costs, and thus, theoretically anyway, improve their profits. Such a model disables the kind of innovation necessary to compete when an industry faces changing consumer demands, as we discussed in Chapter 2, and that is precisely where the appliance portfolio was headed: proliferation, personalization, customization—all antithetical to a well-controlled, long-run, cost-constricted, superefficient manufacturing, marketing, and distribution operation.

So Haier decided to dramatically remake itself. Realizing that successful innovation in the marketplace depended on catering to these shifting consumer demands, Haier restructured its entire business around a concept of "zero distance"—each unit within Haier would be directly in contact with consumers. The company eliminated ten thousand positions in middle management—enough to rattle the conceptual cage and refocus attitudes toward the business—and restructured the majority of their remaining employees into more than four thousand microenterprises (MEs).[10]

It is instructive to think of these MEs—comprised of ten to fifteen people—like start-ups. All MEs are charged with autonomous responsibility for their product, conducting their own market research and setting their own ambitious goals for growth, and they are additionally responsible for developing and strengthening the ecosystem in which that product lives. Such a restructuring allows each ME to ask the essential question raised earlier in this chapter: Why does our product exist? With individual ownership of product design and functionality, each ME is positioned to realize and build its own interaction field. They are able to do this by maintaining zero distance from consumers of their product.

The culmination of this restructuring—as well as the commitment to innovation, collaboration, and customer solutions—can be seen in Haier's establishment of the Haier Open Partnership Ecosystem (HOPE). This online portal connects Haier's MEs with one another, as well as with external business partners, designers, and would-be customers to source ideas for product development and innovation. Through this channel (as well as various social media platforms) Haier generates more than one thousand product ideas from customers every year; some MEs are even led by would-be customers whose exemplary input online earned them positions in the company.[11]

The point about Haier is that any company, no matter how entrenched in the standard value-chain model, has the capacity to become an interaction field company. Removing strata of bureaucracy—only two layers of management divide Haier's CEO from its bottom-level employees—enabled Haier to focus discretely on customer-driven product innovation, innovation that hinges on each product's viability within a market ecosystem. The velocity Haier achieved is a simple lesson in physics: it requires less energy to bring a small mass to the same velocity as a larger mass, because there is less friction to overcome. By eliminating the obstacles of bureaucratic hierarchy, Haier got out of its own way.

In the last decade, Haier has seen profits grow by more than 20 percent per year, with revenue increasing nearly as much. The company has created more than $2 billion in market value and, after the initial layoffs, has created more jobs than it began with as a result of its "rapidly expanding ecosystem."[12] In all of this, Haier stands head and shoulders above its competitors, both international and domestic.

The lesson here is that it is not necessary to dismantle your business enterprise or begin your interaction field journey with massive layoffs; the point is, rather, that it is far easier to launch a satellite into an interaction field than launch an entire planet. Take Alibaba as another example. Although Alibaba is now an enormous interaction field company—a virtual marketplace that provides and hosts all of its own vital services, from computing systems to financial instruments—it began rather humbly as a business-to-business online marketplace with eighteen employees.

Classically a start-up—a microenterprise from the beginning— Alibaba's size at the outset offered flexibility, maneuverability, and rapid adaptation. That is why, once in the virtual marketplace, it was able to explode with such velocity. It saw itself in a much wider field where interactions were taking place—interactions it could be at the center of. In order to do so, it spun off new businesses—Taobao, Tmall, Ant Financial—to achieve and maintain similar velocity in its expanded spaces.

Whether your company is a start-up or more traditional, how it is structured plays a significant role in whether or not it can achieve velocity in the interaction field. A company that is best able to respond to the signals in the noise—by constantly utilizing customer feedback, emphasizing innovation, and promoting the success of the broader interaction field as a whole—will achieve the greatest velocity and see the most success as an interaction field company.

First, you must identify the opportunity of an interaction field. This means uncovering the purpose of your company or product and identifying what problems it helps customers, and the world, solve. It also means figuring out a way to seamlessly intersect in the lives of your nucleus participants, ecosystem participants, and market makers and determining how all the participants in the interaction field collaborate and interact. No one group solves all the problems in isolation. Second, you must structure for velocity. An organization built for velocity in an interaction field will be able to quickly and efficiently utilize data to innovate constantly, both strengthening and increasing the interactions it creates or facilitates within the field.

Measurement of the Interaction Field: Rethinking Growth

I never said that building an interaction field would be easy, only that it could be done. It requires both a kind of enlightenment and a certain amount of risk. You may have to rethink your product or service—how it lives in the world, why it exists, and who it exists for—or you may have to restructure your management. Perhaps it goes without saying at this point, but this reorientation must be done with the perspective of accelerating the velocity of the interactions.

Perhaps this all sounds well and good to you. "OK," you say. "That makes a bit more sense. I can see several possible interaction fields my company can be involved in, and I have a better idea of how to go about it." But you may ask next, "How do I know if I am succeeding? How do I know if I'm about to go bust?"

The question of measurement is an important one, but unfortunately the answer is tricky, and the vital metrics for one interaction field may be quite different from those of another. But the oldest interaction in the history of business—namely, sales—is no longer a sufficient or foundational measure of success. It is, in many respects, the feeblest of all interactions. It is necessary, of course, but it does not guarantee customer retention, innovation, or velocity in the twenty-first century.

In an interaction field company, success is evaluated in part with quantity or frequency measures, such as the number of participants and interactions. But interaction field companies do not merely see numerical growth—in terms of assets amassed, profitability increased, compound annual growth rate improved year after year, return on investment, return on equity—as the goal. The more meaningful metrics are quality measures. These include the speed and scope of the propagation of interactions—what we've been calling velocity—the number, type, and potential of collaboration opportunities that arise and movement into new areas of the field.

As Klöckner learned, companies with interaction fields can scale exponentially. We have seen this kind of mesmerizing, fantastic explosion in presence from Google, Apple, Amazon, and the other leading platform companies. Similarly, the desired outcome of the interaction field model is acceleration through network effects, learning effects, and viral effects, which enable established companies to adapt to rapidly changing markets. These companies scale at a significantly faster rate than value-chain companies.

The interaction field company, then, seeks to achieve velocity to the point that it dominates or even defines a field, as GoPro, Netflix, and others have done. At that point, the traditional ideas of competitive advantage become meaningless. Success is primarily measured in terms of the frequency of a participant taking the single action that most adds value to the interaction field, the speed and scope of propagation, collaboration opportunities, and movement into new areas of the field.

Success for the interaction field company is all about creating new, meaningful, shared, and exponential value, evolving new organization forms, opening new ways forward, and continuously exceeding customer expectations. The interaction field company achieves velocity when its participants embrace the field and through their engagement, which powers a virtuous cycle. The cycle creates momentum and exponential growth through network, learning, and viral effects. Money matters, but it comes along after other measures of success.

Because performance is understood and defined differently in an interaction field, companies will have to rethink, rework, and in some cases abandon the traditional metrics that once indicated success and growth. Although some inherited measures will undoubtedly linger—revenue, share price, profits, and payouts—many will not be calculated in the same ways, such as click counts, daily active users, or volume of commodities purchased or sold.

While some of the integral aspects of a growing and thriving interactional field can be measured—such as the number of members within the nucleus and ecosystem or the average number of interactions between them per day—others are more difficult to calculate, such as the value, meaning, or degree of reciprocity of those interactions. Logging daily active users, for instance, provides data that can be harnessed only when coupled with insight as to how and why they interact. Facebook boasts of daily active users over monthly active users, and Amazon highlights its millions of Prime members, but the lack of insight into the quality of those interactions hinders these companies' ability to attain the self-reinforcing effects of velocity and the exponentiality that leads to a virtuous cycle, one in which companies not only increase revenues for themselves and their participants, but achieve economic development toward a social good.

If, hypothetically, one in ten Facebook users posts "fake news" every day, and two of ten become increasingly disaffected by targeted advertisements and the apparent lack of reciprocity, is Facebook learning anything useful about itself? Can it take advantage of the numbers it counts to unlock potential velocity?

The various components of the interaction field I have discussed—the nucleus, ecosystem, and market makers; the quality of interactions; and the effects of velocity—will all contribute to a new paradigm of business growth, characterized by a new hockey stick, if you will. To draw an example, I will use a prototypical indicator of company success in the retail sector: gross merchandise volume, the standard by which e-commerce retail companies are typically compared.

Amazon launched in 1995 as a seller of books and went public on May 16, 1997. By any measure, Amazon is a successful e-commerce retailer, but, as I have argued, it fails to take advantage of its platform and its participants, and thus misses an opportunity for even greater growth. Only in the last five years has Amazon seen what might best be called its platform effect.

Alibaba was founded in 1999 by a gang of eighteen led by English teacher Jack Ma. If you compare Alibaba to Amazon or any other retailer in terms of GMV, it is apparent that Alibaba is the most successful of all (see Figure 9). But most important are its velocity metrics in the twenty years since the company was founded. The number of active annual users grew 18 percent, to 654 million Chinese consumers, in the quarter ending in March 2019. Active monthly mobile shoppers grew to 721 million, an increase of 22 million in three months and 104 million over the previous year. Interaction velocity increases with the length of time the participant

Figure 9. E-commerce company comparison (GMV in billions USD) 2019
Source: And where does Amazon stand now compared to Alibaba & Co.?, Exciting Commerce (blog), April 11, 2019, https://excitingcommerce.de/2019/04/11/und-wo-steht -amazon-jetzt-im-vergleich-zuz-alibaba-co/.

has been active on Alibaba. Consumers who had been with Alibaba for approximately five years placed an average of 132 orders in twenty-three product categories, while those who had been on Alibaba for only one year placed an average of twenty-seven orders in six product categories. The average annual active consumer placed ninety orders in sixteen product categories.[13] These figures don't count searches and other interactions that take place on Alibaba; they merely capture sales on its marketplace. There is not a marketplace, retailer, or company that has higher interaction velocity at scale than Alibaba, and its future looks brighter than many other companies. In a study of fifty of the companies that are poised for sustained, strong growth—*Fortune*'s "Future 50"—Alibaba ranked number fourteen and was the most valuable company on the list.[14]

Why is that so?

Alibaba operates under nontraditional standards of growth, and it is still expanding its interaction field. It cannot do this in old-school, profit-generating ways, such as simply increasing the range of products or services, acquiring and incorporating competitors, or monopolizing an industry. Interaction field companies seek to transform industries, not master them, and the degree to which Alibaba has facilitated such a transformation while propagating small-business and wholesale economic development cannot be adequately captured by any standard statistic. As Alibaba's interaction field grows, the benefits and value accrue across participants; the growth of every mom-and-pop shop selling on Taobao is the growth of Alibaba, whether or not it is reflected in the e-giant's revenue stream. It is difficult to imagine the potential exponentiality Alibaba will achieve when it attains ample velocity throughout its interaction field to become a kind of virtuoso of business creation and development for a thoroughly integrated commercial world.

If we imagine the new hockey stick, a long period might be spent in slow growth. This is when a company develops its nucleus, engages an ecosystem, and identifies market makers. This nontraditional growth is unlikely to be reflected in traditional measures. Once the interaction field is built out, however, and after it reaches a critical threshold of participants and interactions—in which velocity triggers the effects of virality, network, and learning mechanisms—then the business enters, as if without notice, a stage of exponentiality. It is at this stage that growth skyrockets and the business crosses industries, defies definition, and self-sustains a virtuous cycle that creates opportunity for significant economic and social development and progress.

Numbers in the Interaction Field: Precision Measurement

What is common to all interaction field companies is a healthy obsession with data. They count as much as they can as precisely as they can, even though what they measure is often not clearly linked to what we might call standard measurements of success or growth. Discovery Health, for instance, makes a headline point of how many rewards customers have earned in a week, how many fitness events they have tracked, and how many charitable donations the company's network has bolstered. Not a single one of these interactions puts a dollar in Discovery's pockets, and yet they are a powerful representation of the extent and engagement of the interaction field. They are, respectively, a measure of reciprocity, of meaning, and of Discovery's "social return" or value.

I use this example to make the point that it is important for interaction field companies to count as many interactions as possible, as each data point can potentially serve to expand the field by attracting disparate participants into the ecosystem or to create the kind of network and learning effects that lead to exponentiality. Determining what to count, and for what reasons, depends entirely on the nature of the interaction field and its overarching goals.

The concept of precision is important. The data captured must measure not only the instance of an interaction, but the effects of the interaction as well. It is not enough to know that an interaction occurred. Truly successful interaction field companies collect data that determines why an interaction occurred, how it occurred, and what interactions have resulted as a consequence. This is the nature of the interaction field, where commodities are not simply bought and sold.

Let's remember John Deere and its concept of precision tillage. Deere thinks as much about its machinery and technology as it does about how and where its products are used—that is, on the one hundred million acres of farmland Deere customers tend. The potential insights gleaned from the precision tillage data accumulated with every single seed planted in Deere's interaction field was unimaginable before Deere developed it. A database of real-world agricultural data has the potential to address serious global crises. Theoretically, Deere could map ideal conditions in which to fertilize, plant, and harvest any crop on any acre of farmland in the world. For a single farmer, it might seem overkill to measure seed depth to the millimeter. But when aggregated by an interaction field company, such data is a powerful tool—not only for attracting customers, but for solving immense problems. It is, too, this kind of precision measurement that attracts ecosystem members with a variety of goals, such as reducing herbicides and pesticides, controlling water use, or adjusting cropland to maintain productivity in response to climate change.

A similar effect can be seen with Flatiron Health. Its interaction field depends on the acquisition and incorporation of previously uncounted real-world data and the sharing of that data with the entire interaction field, from the nucleus to the ecosystem to the market makers. After discovering that vital patient information was not being tabulated in electronic health records, Flatiron employed a team of medical and research professionals to work within community cancer clinics and manually log the previously missed data—which they call "unstructured data"—into their system. Despite a heavy expenditure of money and labor hours, such a method—entrusted to credible industry professionals—was vital for the fluent and effective operation of Flatiron's platform. In a 2018 study, researchers found that Flatiron's real-world data—or, they hope to prove one day, real-world *evidence*—drastically improved "sensitivity of mortality information" from electronic health record data, from 66 percent without the unstructured data to 91 percent with it.[15] This staggering success—and the ability to measure it—made Flatiron's partnership with the FDA something of an inevitability.

The partnership, established in January 2018, and its initial success led to the FDA's announcement in December 2018 of a "framework for [a] real-world evidence program." While the program's existence is in itself an indication of the success of Flatiron's recent efforts to move the industry in that direction, the framework also includes a collaboration between the FDA's Oncology Center of Excellence and Flatiron "to examine how RWD [real-world data] can be used to gain insights regarding the safety and effectiveness of new cancer therapies."[16]

It is not a question of simply generating the most data possible, but rather the right data—the kind of data that can provide truly revolutionary insights to solve ambitiously broad goals.

Interactions: Quality Versus Quantity

Yes, the number of interactions is important, but not nearly as important as the quality of those interactions. It is necessary not only to gauge immediate feedback on measures like customer satisfaction but also to identify whether or not certain interactions benefit the interaction field as a whole.

The following infographics from Kloeckner Metals—the US-specific subsidiary of Klöckner & Co.—reveal some of the interaction measures the company tracks on its Part Manager platform, which customers use to browse, select, and stock steel inventory:[17]

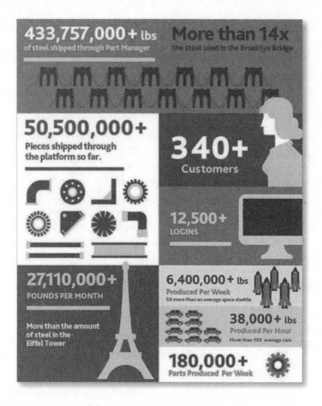

Figure 10. Kloeckner Metals business metrics
Source: "How Ordering Steel Online via Part Manager Brings Happiness," Kloeckner Metals, June 6, 2017.

Kloeckner Metals shows 340 customers, 12,500 log-ins, and 433 million pounds of steel shipped. While these figures indicate a certain strength of the business, they are not, in an interaction field, stand-alone measures of success. The measures that stand out in an interaction field are those that indicate a company's ability to solve problems by reducing frictions and increasing efficiencies.

It is here that the kind of survey data included in the second info-graphic becomes vitally important. More than 90 percent of respondents agreed that the Part Manager "makes their job easier," while 66 percent were able to "reduce their workload" and 60 percent "reduced disruptions in their order process" through the Part Manager portal. In each of these measures there is, undoubtedly, more data to extract, but without

Figure 11. Kloeckner Metals business metrics
Source: "How Ordering Steel Online via Part Manager Brings Happiness," Kloeckner Metals, June 6, 2017.

similarly qualitative feedback, it is difficult to know whether interactions throughout the ecosystem and market are of the quality that self-sustains while generating velocity. It is not enough to ask, "Is my business doing well?" Interaction field companies must ask, "Is my business making a difference?"

In order to appropriately and adequately measure quality, an interaction field company must adopt the perspectives of its participants, each of whom—especially as they come to span broad sectors and industries—engages with the interaction field with a different hierarchy of goals. While keeping the perspective of participants, it is crucial to focus on three elements of the interaction field enterprise we have already discussed: reciprocity, meaning, and value.

How to measure these will depend largely on the nature of the company, the industry or industries it serves, and the hierarchy of goals it has aligned itself with. But the essential elements are the same:

- *Reciprocity.* What do interaction field participants receive in exchange for their engagement?
- *Meaning.* How do we achieve the intent or purpose of the business and brand? How does it solve the multiple and diverse problems and challenges of the interaction field participants?
- *Value.* What new and shared value can be created and scaled exponentially? Are we improving the lives of all participants in the interaction field?

However the measurements are organized or whatever data is collected, measures of success should be approached with these markers in mind.

Three Elements of Performance Evaluation

First, rethink what growth means to your enterprise. Expansion in size may be part of it, but what you're really after is smart growth that reaches through the target space and into others. Second, you must consider the benefit—formerly known as profit—from the perspective of all current and potential participants, who often engage to accomplish a variety of goals. Finally, in order to achieve a virtuous cycle, you need to capture and evaluate data that perpetuates its own development in line with solving higher-order societal and economic problems.

I remember the days when CAGR was king (compound annual growth rate, for those who haven't had the pleasure of encountering it before). In the subsequent era, "shareholder value" was all. We have seen various attempts to bring in the social-value element, through the "triple bottom line" and "B corps," but either they do not fully integrate the levels of solutions or they require such specialist qualifications that most companies will not bother. Besides, neither has much to do with interactions of velocity.

To round off this discussion, it's important to keep in mind that it's not just measurement that's under siege, but capitalism itself, and its focus on money, profit, gain, and winning. According to a study from the Harvard Kennedy School's Institute of Politics, only 42 percent of millennials support capitalism. "Young Americans are sending a strong message," says polling director John Della Volpe. "They care deeply about the future, but are concerned that the current state of our institutions and our politics are not sufficient to meet our nation's challenges."[18]

Counting beans and measuring bottom lines will not bring the next generations into business.

New Ways Forward

The World Is Created Through Interactions

The world is created through interactions.

    Interactions are possible because of the enormous progress we have made in connecting everything: information, data, people, things. In this world of connectivity, interactions are the foundation of value. The greater the quantity and the higher the quality of these interactions, the more they benefit everyone.

This connected world has progressed through three eras of development.[1] In the first, beginning in the early 1990s, the World Wide Web emerged, facilitating search and e-commerce. Google and Amazon were founded during that era and have become the most valuable companies today. During the second era, which began 2007, social media and mobile phones digitized people's behaviors. Apple and Samsung delivered the devices. Facebook and WeChat transformed communication. Uber, Lyft, and Airbnb built on them. A stunning number of service companies emerged, each one referred to as "the Uber of" whatever its industry was.

We are now on the brink of a third era, in which everything will be digitized and connectivity will be ubiquitous, thanks to a new set of technologies. Machine learning will power the connectivity of data.

The Internet of Things will connect everything without requiring human-to-human or human-to-machine interaction. Data transfer over 5G networks will be accomplished at enormous speed. Quantum computing will deliver significant leaps of computer power.

In this era, there will also be new devices and technologies for connectivity. The mobile phone will give way to new user interfaces including voice, video, sensors, natural language, and augmented reality. We are just at the beginning. This third era will have a significant impact on every industry and market category in the world. Just as in previous eras, there will be certain companies that will prosper or even dominate. These powerful new companies will be interaction field enterprises.

We have come through the age of the platform, experienced the era of the ecosystem, and are now entering a period defined by interactions. It is a world that is increasingly a place of vanishing walls and disappearing boundaries.

Just as traditional businesses were disrupted in the second era, now whole industries and categories will radically change and reorder. Competitors emerge from anywhere, including other industries—Tesla into aerospace, Netflix into content creation, Google into mobility. As technologies converge, these borders disappear by democratizing data, shrinking distance, eliminating intermediaries, and empowering consumers, making way for ever escalating customer expectations.

Some observers believe that the new competition is between ecosystems, rather than between companies, but that is not how I see it. Whether it is business ecosystems, digital ecosystems, solutions ecosystems, or transaction ecosystems, such systems are just transitional models, typically evolving from traditional pipeline or platform businesses. I think that more and more interaction fields will develop and companies will seek to build their positions within those fields. That's because only interaction fields can solve the diverse and ephemeral needs of multiple participants: individual goals, category challenges, and larger societal aims. Interaction fields will mash up multiple ecosystems, a sort of system of a system, and value chains will merge with other interaction fields. Participants will engage in complex networks of interaction fields. The interaction field companies will seek to collaborate with each other and to create meaningful, valuable, and reciprocal interactions that produce new and shared value for all. The era of competition as we know it will come to an end.

The entire world economy will be—and already is—transformed and reshaped in profound ways. McKinsey predicts that $60 trillion in revenue, or roughly 30 percent of all global revenues, will be accounted for by interaction field–style ecosystems by 2025.[2] That prediction was made in 2018 and requires updating. One source compares interaction field companies' weekly stock performance with the Dow Jones Industrial Average, Nasdaq Composite, and DAX and shows that they outpace the companies listed on the major stock exchanges significantly.[3]

This is the great opportunity and promise of the interaction field model. Why?

- We live in a world of acceleration—technology, globalization, climate change—and connectivity of everything, and the interaction field model helps to manage such a world.
- The model helps participants compete and collaborate in a world without walls.
- More value is created by platform businesses than by others. Facebook, Amazon, Netflix, Google, and Apple are worth over $3 trillion. In just two years, they have added $1 trillion in market capitalization. Value-chain companies can capture some of this value, not by trying to emulate FANGA, but by leaping into interaction fields.
- A model is urgently needed that solves broad societal challenges while also meeting specific daily goals of consumers.

Some interaction fields are quite narrow in scope, with a relatively well defined and homogeneous set of participants in the nucleus. Klöckner's participants are all members of the steel community. GoPro's all have adventure in their blood. Other interaction fields are much broader. An Alibaba participant is almost anyone who shops for almost anything.

Some interaction field companies develop very open platforms, while others keep them quite closed. This decision can pose a challenge. As described in a World Economic Forum report, "Opening too little means that third parties cannot participate and add value. Opening too much means loss of control, inability to steer the community and inability to monetize. The most successful platforms start with a few key partners, who build critical apps on top, then open more over time." This is just what we saw Klöckner do. John Deere has a remarkably open platform, welcoming in a range of partners and competitors to the ecosystem and including influencers and observers as market makers. Apple, by contrast, is quite closed but may have to gradually open up as its gravitational pull weakens.

The number of participants varies from company to company, and the sheer volume of participants cannot be considered as a measure of success. Klöckner and GoPro are small. Alibaba is huge. It is about the quality of interactions and the network, viral, and learning effects.

Whatever the shape and size, as I have stressed, the interaction field model is the only system that will thrive in this third era. That is because it is the only model that can continuously evolve, helping companies to respond to ever rising customer expectations. The more velocity the interaction field takes on, the more value-creating the system becomes.

The interaction field model enables companies to improve automatically. The more interactions, the more value is created, because they make the system more precise. For John Deere, as farmers contribute data daily, the interaction field continuously improves the accuracy of fertilizing and seeding. Value-chain companies may claim to achieve continuous improvement, but, even if they do, those changes will necessarily be slower and less comprehensive than those of interaction field companies.

The interaction field company becomes ultra-flexible and can constantly adapt to changing markets or conditions. Consider John Deere again. Let's assume that a new bacteria appears on some farms and kills a crop. If farmers share the data, Deere is the first to know about the problem, since it has comparative data from many farms. It can immediately go out and find solutions to counteract the bacteria. It can identify another pesticide to make available to the participants or initiate research with one or more pesticide companies. This benefits the farmer participants, of course, but also Deere, because it gets a cut from the pesticide sales, just as Amazon gets a cut from the sales of a third-party seller. Deere can thus add new revenue streams based on whatever is happening in the interaction field. The company becomes, in other words, the ultimate learning organization. The days of market research, customer surveys, and online ratings will come to an end.

Much like solving the challenges of a new bacteria in agriculture, a properly designed interaction field can solve much larger challenges such as the spreading coronavirus that causes the COVID-19 disease today.

How else can a company, industry, or society deal with the chaotic, mercurial business and social environment we live and do business in? Platforms are not enough. Transactions are not enough. Yes, Uber gets the data from riders about where they want to be picked up and where they want to go—which enables the company to optimize the location of its drivers—but that's about it. Nor is a platform plus an ecosystem enough. It helps you to improve the product a bit more and make the experience more seamless, but not much else.

Only if you have all three elements of the interaction field—and you have configured and composed them in a way that powers a virtuous cycle fed with interactions—does the system update itself automatically. Only then is knowledge applied. Only then does a company fully help its participants achieve their goals, from the most individual challenges to the most global, difficult to solve, and intractable problems of our society, today and in the future.

Interaction fields are the future, not only of business, but of the world.

Acknowledgments

"If I have seen further than others, it is by standing on the shoulders of giants," said Isaac Newton. This quote comes to my mind as I am thinking about what got me here, finishing my third book.

I am standing on the shoulders of many giants. I have been incredibly blessed with working with many, many executives, teams of executives, and companies who have invited me or my company, Vivaldi Group, to work inside their companies and help them solve innovation, brand, marketing, and growth challenges they face.

I also have been part of a large global community of academics from various fields who encouraged, motivated, and inspired me over the years, first at the University of Kansas, and later during my academic career at the Harvard Business School, IESE Business School, and the Darden School of the University of Virginia.

There are several streams of scientific and academic research that have strongly influenced me and the writing in this book. First are the academics from strategy who helped me understand how the nature of competitive advantage has been changing over time, such as Michael Porter or Rita Gunther McGrath. Three academics, David Collis and the late Michael Rukstad of the Harvard Business School, and the late Paddy Miller of IESE Business School, have been also lifelong friends and collaborators. Second are the group of academics who have done some of the best writing in the areas of digital platforms and ecosystems, such as Geoffrey G. Parker, Marshall W. Van Alstyne, Sangeet Paul Choudary, David S. Evans, David B. Yoffie, Annabelle Gawer, Melissa Schilling, and Michael G. Jacobides. Third are the group of sociologists and psychologists who study how people join social networks, how social behaviors spread, or who study the cognitive biases that affect relationships or interactions between people and social influence. These scholars include Daniel Kahneman, Richard Thaler, Nichola Christakis, James H. Fowler, Dirk Helbing, Jonah Berger, and Paul J. Zak.

An important area of influence in writing this book has been my good friends and colleagues in the fields of marketing, consumer behavior, and branding, particularly David A. Aaker, Professor Emeritus at the University of California, Berkeley's Haas School of Business, and Kevin Lane Keller, the E. B. Osborn Professor of Marketing at the Tuck School of Business at Dartmouth College. Dave and Kevin have been an inspiration for my continued interest in how strong brands are built and how consumers connect with brands, along with the giants of marketing, such as Gary Lilien, Philip Kotler, George Day, and Yoram Wind.

There is a large number of people who work at the intersection of business and academia who strongly influenced this book as well, some are close friends. Authors, writers, and thinkers, such as Haydn Shaughnessy, Salim Ismail, Azeem Azhar, Peter C. Evans, Konstantinos Apostolatos, Mark Ritson, John Hagel, Tom Goodwin, Marc Bonchek, Matthias Walter, Andrew Chen, Dr. Holger Schmidt, Simone Cicero, J. P. Kuehlwein, Thomas Wedell-Wedellsborg, Peter Schumacher, Nir Eyal, Dirk Notheis, Eric Noel, Darren Coleman, Simon Torrance, James Currier, Anand Sanwal, Ralph Oliva, and Benedict Evans.

I am indebted to these giants on whose shoulders I am standing.

A special thanks go to the wonderful community, or shall I say, family of Vivaldians at Vivaldi Group. Over twenty years now I have worked with some of the most terrific strategy consultants, creatives, marketers, thought leaders, researchers, platform thinkers, technologists, engineers, game changers, and design thinkers who have welcomed me, challenged me intellectually and professionally, and improved my work daily: Anne Olderog, Larry Lucas, Björn Sander, Marc Scherer, Steve Firth, Andrew Roberts, Lee Powney, German Yunes, Luis Gerardin, Alberto Velasco,

Pete Killian, Sara Riis, and Agathe Blanchon, to point out just the most senior partners and friends. But above all are three amazing and talented individuals: Richard Rolka, the most fearless leader at Vivaldi; Tom Ajello, a creative digital technology guru and master designer; and Dr. Markus Zinnebauer, one of the best strategists and senior consultants. Richard, Tom, and Markus are truly three of the most incredible professionals in the consulting business that are always close by me. And I cannot forget to mention the most wonderful person in the Vivaldi world that makes "the machine" run smoothly, Anneth Pablo.

A special thanks goes to the wonderful people at PublicAffairs, especially Colleen Lawrie, my editor, who provided thoughtful feedback and comments and shaped the manuscript in so many important ways; Kelly Lenkevich, the production editor; and Elizabeth Dana, the copyeditor. A huge thanks goes to Esmond Harmsworth of Aevitas Creative Management, my agent for over fifteen years, who had trust in me, and whose wonderful and delightful ways have kept this author on course over the years.

Many authors will attest to the lonely journey of writing a book, but I have been incredibly lucky to have been introduced to John Butman, an American author, editor, and one of the most prolific writers. With John, the journey hasn't been a lonely one. His wit and personality made the journey enjoyable. His thoughtful critique and frank and direct feedback and superb writing skills made the book what it is now. Thank you.

Notes

Chapter One: The Interaction Field Model

1. This new business model and its evolution toward a digital ecosystem has been comprehensively discussed in several award-winning publications, including Marshall W. Van Alstyne, Geoffrey G. Parker, and Sangeet Paul Choudary, "Pipeline, Platforms, and the New Rules of Strategy," *Harvard Business Review*, April 2017; Geoffrey G. Parker, Marshall W. Van Alstyne, and Sangeet Paul Choudary, *Platform Revolution: How Networked Markets Are Transforming the Economy and How to Make Them Work for You* (New York: W. W. Norton, 2016).

2. Michael G. Jacobides, Arun Sundararajan, and Marshall W. Van Alstyne, eds., *Platforms and Ecosystems: Enabling the Digital Economy* (briefing paper, World Economic Forum, Geneva, Switzerland, February 2019), 12.

3. Erin Griffith, "Bird Is Said to Raise New Funding at $2.5 Billion Valuation," *New York Times*, July 22, 2019, www.nytimes.com/2019/07/22/technology /bird-scooters-valuation.html.

4. Here an explanation of indirect (or cross-side network effects) versus direct network effects, where users benefit from other users joining the platform. Riders of Uber don't benefit from having more riders join the Uber platform. Similarly, drivers don't benefit from more drivers. There are some indirect network effects: the more drivers join Uber, the lower the estimated time of pick up for riders. This effect, however, is also limited because users don't care much between a pickup within five minutes versus three minutes.

5. Jasmine Wu, "There Are Now 175 Online Mattress Companies—and You Can't Tell Them Apart," CNBC, August 18, 2019, www.cnbc.com/2019/08/18 /there-are-now-175-online-mattress-companiesand-you-cant-tell-them-apart .html.

6. Barry Schwartz, *The Paradox of Choice: Why More Is Less* (New York: Ecco, 2004).

7. "Amazon.com Market Cap:1.020T for Feb. 4, 2020," YCharts, accessed February 5, 2020, https://ycharts.com/companies/AMZN/market_cap.

8. Alexis C. Madrigal, "The Servant Economy," *Atlantic*, March 6, 2019, www.theatlantic.com/technology/archive/2019/03/what-happened-uber-x-companies/584236/.

9. Marshall W. Van Alstyne, "The Opportunity and Challenge of Platforms," in *Platforms and Ecosystems: Enabling the Digital Economy*, ed. Michael G. Jacobides, Arun Sundararajan, and Marshall W. Van Alstyne (briefing paper, World Economic Forum, Geneva, Switzerland, February 2019), 9.

10. I call it the nucleus because, in the case of the interaction field, the producer is also the platform builder, orchestrator, or owner. It is a special case of a platform. In the more typical case of a platform or two-sided marketplace, the platform owner, builder, or orchestrator is different from the producer. In the example of Uber, the Uber company is the platform owner, builder, and orchestrator, but the producers are the hundreds of thousands of drivers offering rides.

11. Kevin Kelly, "AR Will Spark the Next Big Tech Platform—Call It Mirror World," *Wired*, February 12, 2019.

12. Haydn Shaughnessy, "What Is Value-Based Agile?," *Medium*, May 10, 2019.

Chapter Two: Revolutionizing a Company and Industry

1. Scott Ferguson, "John Deere Bets the Farm on AI, IoT," *Light Reading*, March 12, 2018.

2. Jacob Bunge, "Supersized Family Farms Are Gobbling Up American Agriculture," *Wall Street Journal*, October 23, 2017, www.wsj.com/articles/the-family-farm-bulks-up-1508781895.

3. Alex Konrad, "How Farmers Business Network Plans to Disrupt Big Agra, One Farm at a Time," *Forbes*, March 7, 2017, www.forbes.com/sites/alexkonrad/2017/03/07/farmers-business-network-takes-on-big-agra-with-funding-from-gv/#1d36a2535d86.

4. Elizabeth Dunn, "Seeds of a Better Business," *Bloomberg Businessweek*, March 11, 2019, 18–19.

5. Andrew Noel, "A Bumper Crop of Information," *Bloomberg Businessweek*, March 15, 2019, 47–48.

6. "FarmBeats: AI, Edge & IoT for Agriculture," Microsoft, May 14, 2015, www.microsoft.com/en-us/research/project/farmbeats-iot-agriculture/.

7. Alexia Fernández Campbell, "Food Stamps Helped Lift the US Economy out of the Great Recession," *Vox*, June 5, 2019, www.vox.com/2019/6/5/18650437/usda-snap-food-stamps-economic-impact.

8. Josh Wilson, "Feeding the Future: Fixing the World's Faulty Food System," *Telegraph*, www.telegraph.co.uk/news/feeding-the-future/.

Chapter Three: New Consumers

1. I will show later how Alibaba has built an interaction field that continuously evolves to serve new needs, moving from e-commerce to finance to logistics, to interact ever more deeply in the lives of consumers and solving needs including travel, health care, culture and entertainment, mobility, and education. Joydeep Sengupta et al., *The Ecosystem Playbook: Winning in a World of Ecosystems* (New York: McKinsey & Company, 2019), 10.

2. James Melton, "Online Retail Sales in China Grew Nearly 24% in 2018, Its Government Says," *Digital Commerce 360*, January 24, 2019; Kirti Vashee, "The Global eCommerce Opportunity Enabled by MT," *eMpTy Pages* (blog), December 25, 2018, http://kv-emptypages.blogspot.com/2018/12/the-global -ecommerce-opportunity.html.

3. Ming Zeng, "Alibaba and the Future of Business," *Harvard Business Review*, September–October 2018, https://hbr.org/2018/09/alibaba-and-the -future-of-business. Ming Zeng is the chair of the Academic Council of the Alibaba Group and the author of *Smart Business: What Alibaba's Success Reveals About the Future of Strategy* (Boston, MA: Harvard Business Review Press, 2018), from which some of the material in this section is drawn.

4. Zeng, *Smart Business*, 219.

5. "Sell on Alibaba.com," https://seller.alibaba.com/memberships/index .html.

6. Aashish Pahwa, "Alibaba Business Model: How Does Alibaba Make Money?," *Feedough*, April 3, 2019, www.feedough.com/alibaba-business -model-how-does-alibaba-make-money/.

7. Jeff Beer, "Alibaba CMO Says Don't Compare the Chinese Company to Amazon. It's Much Bigger," *Fast Company*, June 21, 2017, www.fastcompany .com/40434109/alibaba-cmo-says-dont-compare-the-chinese-company-to -amazon-its-much-bigger.

8. Joe Tsai, "Investments, Acquisitions, Capital Allocation" (PowerPoint presentation, Alibaba 2017 Investor Day, Hangzhou, China, June 8–9, 2017), www.alibabagroup.com/en/ir/presentations/Investments_Acquisitions_and _Capital_Allocation.pdf.

9. Adam Levy, "The 7 Largest E-Commerce Companies in the World," *Motley Fool*, August 23, 2019, www.fool.com/investing/2018/12/26/the-7-largest -e-commerce-companies-in-the-world.aspx.

10. It is interesting to evaluate the differences between Amazon and Alibaba in terms of how they generate interaction velocity. Both companies emphasize the volume or frequency of interactions, but Alibaba has much higher quality of interactions and engagement. See, Eric Gervet et al., *The Platform Imperative* (Chicago, IL: A. T. Kearney, 2019), 3, www.atkearney.co/consumer-goods /article/?/a/the-platform-imperative.

11. Zeng, "Future of Business."

12. John Detrixhe, "China's Ant Financial Raised Almost as Much Money as All US and European Fintech Firms Combined," *Quartz*, January 30, 2019, https://qz.com/1537638/ant-financial-raised-almost-as-much-money-in-2018 -as-all-fintechs-in-us-and-europe/.

13. Beer, "Alibaba CMO Says Don't Compare."

14. Alibaba, "Alibaba Launches A100 Strategic Partnership Program," news release, January 11, 2019, www.alibabagroup.com/en/news/article?news =p190111.

15. Alibaba, "A100 Strategic Partnership Program."

16. Alibaba, "A100 Strategic Partnership Program."

17. Robin Kiera, "WeChat Gives Glimpse into the Future of Banking," *Financial Brand*, April 19, 2018, https://thefinancialbrand.com/72124 /wechat-banking-payments-digital-messaging/.

18. Adam Lashinsky, "Ma vs. Ma," *Fortune*, July 3, 2018, 80.

19. As illustrated by Salim Ismail of Singularity University. See, Alina Siegfried, "Mind Altering Substance: Exponential Technology with Salim Ismail," Medium, July 31, 2015, https://stories.ehf.org/mind-altering-substance -exponential-technology-with-salim-ismail-23f36a73313f.

Chapter Four: Framing and Branding

1. *LEGO Play Well Report 2018* (Billund, Denmark: Lego Foundation, 2018).

2. Chris Higgins, "How Many Combinations Are Possible Using 6 LEGO Bricks?," *Mental Floss*, February 12, 2017, http://mentalfloss.com/article/92127 /how-many-combinations-are-possible-using-6-LEGO-bricks.

3. Lars Silberbauer, "LEGO Group Is Still the Most Digital Engaging Brand," August 17, 2016, www.larssilberbauer.com/single-post/2016/08/07 /LEGO-Group-Still-Most-Digital-Engaging-Brand.

4. The Reputation Institute's 2018 survey attributed the Danish toy manufacturer's success to its "strong commitment" to building a corporate brand, as well as its corporate social responsibility and sense of purpose, evidenced by launches like its line of eco-friendly sugarcane bricks. The study is based on more than eighty-seven thousand individual ratings from the general public across Germany, France, Spain, Italy, and the United Kingdom assessing more than 140 multinationals. See Reputation Institute, "Lego Is Most Reputable Company in 2018 Across EU5 Countries Germany, France, Spain, Italy and UK," news release, September 20, 2018, www.globenewswire.com /news-release/2018/09/20/1573451/0/en/Lego-is-Most-Reputable-Company -in-2018-Across-EU5-Countries-Germany-France-Spain-Italy-and-UK .html.

5. An example is Brickworld or the Brickcan (www.brickcan.com/) convention, which invites the public to observe hundreds of LEGO creations and vote for the People's Choice builder award.

6. "Adult Fans of LEGO," Reddit, www.reddit.com/r/AFOL/; "London AFOLs—Adult Fans of Lego," Meetup, www.meetup.com/LondonAFOLs/; London AFOLs, http://londonafols.uk/; Brickish: The UK Club for Adult LEGO Fans, https://brickish.org/; Sam Belkacemi, "For Adults Only: LEGO for Grown-Ups Comes to Intu Trafford Centre," *I Love MCR*, December 5, 2017, https://ilovemanchester.com/adult-only-LEGOland-discovery-manchester/.

7. Conversation with Lars Silberbauer, Vivaldi Platform workshop, November 2018.

8. Data retrieved from Trackalytics (www.trackalytics.com/) on August 15, 2019.

9. Hasan Jensen, "10K Club Interview: Meet Matthew, Mark & Valerie of SpaceX BFR Starship & Super Heavy 1:110 Scale," *LEGO Ideas* (blog), https://ideas.LEGO.com/blogs/a4ae09b6-0d4c-4307-9da8-3ee9f3d368d6/post/64ec13ca-2219-42ef-9fc0-e6576f527ed9.

10. "Women of NASA," Product Idea, LEGO Ideas, last updated August 2, 2016, https://ideas.lego.com/projects/388ddbe3-2f0a-42fb-9f54-93bf3b5f4fe9/updates.

11. The domain of the interaction field is similar to the thinking of Rita McGrath on arenas.

12. Erich Joachimsthaler, "Reframing the Opportunity Space," in *Hidden in Plain Sight: How to Find and Execute Your Company's Next Big Growth Strategy* (Boston, MA: Harvard Business School Press, 2007), 85–109; Thomas Wedell-Wedellsborg, "Are You Solving the Right Problems?," *Harvard Business Review*, January–February 2017, https://hbr.org/2017/01/are-you-solving-the-right-problems.

13. Theodore Levitt, "Marketing Myopia," *Harvard Business Review*, July–August 2004, https://hbr.org/2004/07/marketing-myopia.

14. "Highlights from the February 2020 Farm Income Forecast," USDA Economic Research Service, last updated February 5, 2020, www.ers.usda.gov/topics/farm-economy/farm-sector-income-finances/highlights-from-the-farm-income-forecast/.

15. Paul J. Zak, *The Moral Molecule: The Source of Love and Prosperity* (New York: Dutton, 2012).

16. Nicholas A. Christakis and James H. Fowler, *Connected: The Surprising Power of Our Social Networks and How They Shape Our Lives—How Your Friends' Friends' Friends Affect Everything You Feel, Think, and Do* (New York: Little, Brown Spark, 2009).

17. Mark Earls, *Herd: How to Change Mass Behavior by Harnessing Our True Nature* (Chichester, UK: Wiley, 2009), 127.

18. "Worn Wear," Patagonia, https://wornwear.patagonia.com/.

19. Nicholas A. Christakis and James H. Fowler, *Connected: The Surprising Power of Our Social Networks and How They Shape Our Lives* (New York: Little, Brown Spark, 2011), 12.

Chapter Five: Innovation

1. "Management Board," Klöckner & Co., www.kloeckner.com/en/group /management-board.html.

2. "Crude Steel Production in Major Producing Countries and Regions in 2018," Statista, July 2019, www.statista.com/statistics/267263/world-crude -steel-production-by-region/.

3. Gisbert Rühl, "Disrupting the Steel Industry Through Platforms" (PowerPoint presentation, B2B Online 2018, May 8, 2018), https://slideslive .com/38907723/disrupting-the-steel-industry-through-platforms.

4. Rik Kirkland, "How a Steel Company Embraced Digital Disruption," *McKinsey Quarterly*, May 2016.

5. Marek Sacha, "B2B: XOM Materials," video, filmed at Web Summit 2018, November 5–8, 2018, Lisbon, Portugal, posted November 22, 2018, www.youtube.com/watch?v=5RU6OmldzPE.

6. Rühl, "Disrupting the Steel Industry."

Chapter Six: Solving Difficult Challenges

1. "Workplace Health Glossary: Glossary Terms," Workplace Health Promotion, Centers for Disease Control and Prevention, last updated July 23, 2019, www.cdc.gov/workplacehealthpromotion/tools-resources/glossary/glossary .html.

2. Adrian Gore, "How Discovery Keeps Innovating," *McKinsey Quarterly*, May 2015.

3. Gore, "How Discovery."

4. "Health Insurance Glossary," eHealth, www.ehealthinsurance.com/health -insurance-glossary/.

5. "What We Do," US Food and Drug Administration, last updated March 28, 2018, www.fda.gov/aboutfda/whatwedo/.

6. Hugh Terry, "Discovery Health Vitality Wellness Program," *Digital Insurer*, accessed February 19, 2020, www.the-digital-insurer.com/dia/discovery-health -vitality-wellness-program/.

7. Adrian Gore, "How the Powerful Science of Behaviour Change Can Make Us Healthier," World Economic Forum, November 28, 2018, www.weforum.org/agenda/2018/11/science-incentivize-behaviour-change -vitality-physical-exercise/.

8. Gore, "How Discovery."

9. Discovery Limited, "South Africa's Discovery Sets Ambition to Make 10 Million People Healthier by 2018," news release, September 17, 2018.

10. Discovery, "Vitality-Linked Insurers to Get 100 Million People 20% More Active by 2025," news release, November 28, 2018, www.mynewsdesk .com/za/discovery-holdings-ltd/pressreleases/vitality-linked-insurers-to-get -100-million-people-20-percent-more-active-by-2025-2805513.

11. "Flatiron Health," case study, Amazon Web Services, 2017, https://aws.amazon.com/solutions/case-studies/flatiron-health/.

12. Katherine Noyes, "Flatiron Health's Bold Proposition to Fight Cancer with Big Data," *Fortune*, June 12, 2014, http://fortune.com/2014/06/12/Flatiron-healths-bold-proposition-to-fight-cancer-with-big-data/.

13. Vanessa Candeias et al., "How to Unleash the Enormous Power of Global Healthcare Data," World Economic Forum, December 18, 2018, www.weforum.org/agenda/2018/12/global-healthcare-data-is-a-vast-untapped-resource-until-now/.

14. Amazon Web Services, "Flatiron Health"; Saurav Patyal, "Flatiron Health—Solving Cancer Through Data Analytics," Harvard Business School Digital Innovation and Transformation, April 9, 2018, https://digit.hbs.org/submission/Flatiron-health-solving-cancer-through-data-analytics/.

15. Bobby Daly and Josyula Sowmya, "Why Did Roche Pay $2B for an Oncology Healthcare Start-Up and What Does It Mean for Oncologists?," *JCO OP DAiS* (blog), May 8, 2018, https://jopblog.org/blog/2018/5/8/why-did-roche-pay-2b-for-an-oncology-healthcare-start-up-and-what-does-it-mean-for-oncologists.

16. Vivaldi graphic about Flatiron Health.

17. Saurav Patyal, "Flatiron Health."

18. Reenita Das, "The Flatiron Health Acquisition Is a Shot in the Arm for Roche's Oncology Real-World Evidence Needs," *Forbes*, February 26, 2018, www.forbes.com/sites/reenitadas/2018/02/26/flatiron-health-acquisition-a-shot-in-the-arm-for-roches-oncology-real-world-evidence-needs/#59164f243f60; David Shaywitz, "The Deeply Human Core of Roche's $2.1 Billion Tech Acquisition—and Why It Made It," *Forbes*, February 18, 2018, www.forbes.com/sites/davidshaywitz/2018/02/18/the-deeply-human-core-of-roches-2-1b-tech-acquisition-and-why-they-did-it/#715440cb29c2.

19. Candeias et al., "Enormous Power of Global Healthcare Data."

Chapter Seven: The Virtuous Cycle

1. The metaphor of gravity and gravitational pull in digital strategy has been used previously by Mark Bonchek, "A Good Digital Strategy Creates a Gravitational Pull," *Harvard Business Review*, January 25, 2017.

2. "GoPro with Founder/Inventor Nick Woodman," Malakye, May 1, 2010, www.malakye.com/news/3518/gopro-with-founder-inventor-nick-woodman.

3. Madeline Stone, "The Awesome Life of GoPro's Nick Woodman, America's Highest-Paid CEO," *Business Insider*, April 28, 2015, www.businessinsider.com/life-of-gopro-ceo-nick-woodman-2015-4.

4. Pete Pachal, "To Reboot GoPro, CEO Nick Woodman Went Back to Basics," *Mashable*, December 21, 2018, https://mashable.com/article/nick-woodman-gopro-ceo-talks-hero-7-black-drone-fusion-mashtalk/#of4mu6AKDPqN.

5. Malcolm Gladwell, "The Tipping Point," *New Yorker*, May 27, 1996; Malcolm Gladwell, *The Tipping Point: How Little Things Can Make a Big Difference* (New York: Little, Brown, 2000).

6. Jonah Berger, *Contagious: Why Things Catch On* (New York: Simon & Schuster, 2016).

7. *Social Currency: Why Brands Need to Build and Nurture Social Currency* (New York: Vivaldi Partners, 2010), https://images.fastcompany.com/Vivaldi Partners_SocialCurrency.pdf.

8. "Five Steps for Consumer Brands to Earn Social Currency," *Fast Company*, May 1, 2010, www.fastcompany.com/1615209/five-steps-consumer-brands-earn -social-currency.

9. GoPro, "GoProp: Seagull Stole My GoPro," YouTube video, posted September 30, 2015, www.youtube.com/watch?v=UYHjyNNy_4Y.

10. Ron Ref, Michael Heald, Olivier Jankelovic, "Your Role in the Ecosystem" (Dublin, Ireland: Accenture Strategy, 2017), www.accenture.com/_acn media/pdf-56/accenture-strategy-your-role-in-the-ecosystem.pdf#zoom=50.

11. Joachimsthaler, *Hidden in Plain Sight*.

Chapter Eight: Superfluid Markets

1. "Architects and Architecture," in *The Harper Book of Quotations*, 3rd ed., ed. Robert I. Fitzhenry (New York: Collins Reference, 1993), 41.

2. Talon Homer, "Toyota President Says the Automaker Needs a Redesign," *Drive*, May 9, 2018, www.thedrive.com/news/20728/toyota-president-looks -forward-during-end-of-year-conference.

3. Thomas Koulopoulos with George Achillias, *Revealing the Invisible: How Our Hidden Behaviors Are Becoming the Most Valuable Commodity of the 21st Century* (New York: Post Hill Press, 2018), 145–146; John Voelcker, "1.2 Billion Vehicles on World's Roads Now, 2 Billion by 2035: Report," Green Car Reports, July 29, 2014, www.greencarreports.com/news/1093560_1-2-billion -vehicles-on-worlds-roads-now-2-billion-by-2035-report.

4. INRIX, "INRIX: Congestion Costs Each American 97 hours, $1,348 A Year," news release, February 11, 2019, http://inrix.com/press-releases/scorecard -2018-us/.

5. James Arbib and Tony Seba, *Rethinking Transportation 2020-2030* (San Francisco, RethinkX, 2017), 16, https://static1.squarespace.com/static /585c3439be65942f022bbf9b/t/59f279b3652deaab9520fba6/1509063126843 /RethinkX+Report_102517.pdf.

6. "Car Emissions and Global Warming," Union of Concerned Scientists, July 18, 2014, www.ucsusa.org/clean-vehicles/car-emissions-and-global-warming.

7. "Vehicles, Air Pollution, and Human Health," Union of Concerned Scientists, July 18, 2014, www.ucsusa.org/clean-vehicles/vehicles-air-pollution -and-human-health.

8. "Road Traffic Injuries," World Health Organization, December 7, 2018, www.who.int/en/news-room/fact-sheets/detail/road-traffic-injuries.

9. Matthias Kässer, Thibaut Müller, and Andreas Tschiesner, "Competing in a World of Digital Ecosystems," *McKinsey Quarterly*, February 2018.

10. Wikipedia, s.v. "Hype Cycle," last modified February 8, 2020, 20:34, https://en.wikipedia.org/wiki/Hype_cycle.

11. The think tank CB Insights rates the adoption of auto and mobility trends on three dimensions: the momentum of start-ups in the space, media attention of topic, and customer adoption such as partnerships or customer licensing deals.

12. The dimensions of market strengths are: market sizing forecasts, quality and number of investors, investments in research and development, earning transcript commentary, competitive intensity, and incumbent dealmaking.

13. *The Future of the Automotive Value Chain: 2025 and Beyond* (Munich, Germany: Deloitte, 2017), www2.deloitte.com/content/dam/Deloitte/us /Documents/consumer-business/us-auto-the-future-of-the-automotive-value -chain.pdf.

14. Whim, https://whimapp.com/.

15. Felix Kuhnert, Christoph Stürmer, and Alex Koster, *Five Trends Transforming the Automotive Industry* (Berlin, Germany: Pricewaterhouse-Coopers GmbH Wirtschaftsprüfungsgesellschaft, 2018), www.pwc.at /de/publikationen/branchen-und-wirtschaftsstudien/easy-five-trends -transforming-the-automotive-industry_2018.pdf; Kässer, Müller, and Tschiesner, "Digital Ecosystems."

16. *Electric Vehicles for Smarter Cities: The Future of Energy and Mobility* (Geneva, Switzerland: World Economic Forum, 2018), 5, www3.weforum.org /docs/WEF_2018_%20Electric_For_Smarter_Cities.pdf.

17. Jeff Desjardins, "Electric Vehicles Should Overtake Traditional Sales in Just 20 Years," World Economic Forum, October 1, 2018, www.weforum.org /agenda/2018/10/visualizing-the-rise-of-the-electric-vehicle/.

18. *The Race for the Electric Car* (New York: CB Insights, 2019), 9.

19. Amanda Cooper and Christopher Johnson, "Now Near 100 Million bpd, When Will Oil Peak?," Reuters, September 20, 2018, www .reuters.com/article/us-oil-demand-peak/now-near-100-million-bpd-when -will-oil-demand-peak-idUSKCN1M01TC.

20. "Elon Musk," Tesla, www.tesla.com/elon-musk.

21. Stephen Lacey, "What's Up with Tesla Energy?," *Greentech Media*, March 12, 2019, www.greentechmedia.com/articles/read/whats-up-with-tesla -energy.

22. The origin of the name Uber comes from one of the founders liking the song "California Über Alles" by anti-government band the Dead Kennedys, an allusion to the forbidden first stanza of the national anthem of Germany.

23. David Z. Morris, "Today's Cars Are Parked 95% of the Time," *Fortune*, March 13, 2016, https://fortune.com/2016/03/13/cars-parked-95-percent -of-time/.

24. Darrell Etherington and Lora Kolodny, "Google's Self-Driving Car Unit Becomes Waymo," *TechCrunch*, December 13, 2016, https://techcrunch .com/2016/12/13/googles-self-driving-car-unit-spins-out-as-waymo/.

25. Kirsten Korosec, "Waymo Plans to Open a Self-Driving Car Factory in Michigan," *TechCrunch*, January 22, 2019, https://techcrunch.com/2019/01 /22/waymo-plans-to-open-a-self-driving-car-factory-in-michigan/.

26. Jeb Su, "Tesla CEO Reiterates Plan to Take on Uber, Lyft with Its Own Autonomous Ridesharing Service," *Forbes*, October 25, 2018, www.forbes .com/sites/jeanbaptiste/2018/10/25/tesla-ceo-reiterates-plan-to-take-on-uber -lyft-with-autonomous-ridesharing-service/#543910d699d9.

27. Karla Lant, "By 2023, Tesla Could Have Millions of Cars on the Road," Futurism.com, September 27, 2017, https://futurism.com/by-2023-tesla-could- have-millions-of-cars-on-the-road; Fred Lambert, "Tesla Has Now Deployed Over 10,000 Superchargers Around the World," Electrek, June 9, 2018, https:// electrek.co/2018/06/09/tesla-10000-superchargers/.

28. "Advanced Technologies Group," Uber, www.uber.com/info/atg/.

29. "Identifying Value at Stake for Society and Industry," World Economic Forum, http://reports.weforum.org/digital-transformation/identifying -value-at-stake-for-society-and-industry/.

30. Arbib and Seba, *Rethinking Transportation*, 7.

31. Arbib and Seba, *Rethinking Transportation*, 18.

32. Arbib and Seba, *Rethinking Transportation*, 9.

33. Arbib and Seba, *Rethinking Transportation*, 7–8.

Chapter Nine: Delivering Customer Experiences

1. "Our History," Burberry, https://us.burberry.com/our-history/.

2. Mark Ritson, "Burberry Has a Big Brand Challenge to Replace Christopher Bailey," *Marketing Week*, November 1, 2017.

3. *Digital Transformation: An Interview with Angela Ahrendts* (Paris, France: Capgemini Consulting, 2012), www.capgemini.com/wp-content /uploads/2017/07/DIGITAL_LEADERSHIP__An_interview_with_Angela _Ahrendts.pdf.

4. "Gogoboi Ye Si," *Business of Fashion*, www.businessoffashion.com /community/people/gogoboi-ye-si.

5. Limei Hoang, "How Burberry Is Operationalizing 'See Now, Buy Now,'" *Business of Fashion*, September 17, 2016.

6. *The Future of Fashion: From Design to Merchandising, How Tech Is Reshaping the Industry* (New York: CB Insights, 2019).

7. *Future of Fashion.*

8. Imran Amed et al., *The State of Fashion 2019* (London: Business of Fashion and McKinsey & Company), 17.

9. Amed et al., *The State of Fashion 2019*.

10. Amed et al., *The State of Fashion 2019*, 48.

11. Amed et al., *The State of Fashion 2019*, 47.

12. Olivia Singer, "5 Things to Know About Riccardo Tisci's Debut Burberry Collection," *Vogue Britain*, September 18, 2018, www.vogue.co.uk/gallery/burberry-ss19-riccardo-tisci-debut-everything-you-need-to-know.

Chapter Ten: Velocity Versus Clicks

1. Cadie Thompson, "The Company Behind Some of the Most Popular Candies in the World Is Quietly Taking Over the Pet-Care Industry," *Business Insider*, January 13, 2018.

2. Market Research Future, "Pet Care Market Had Valued at Approximately US$75 BN During the Forecast Period (2017–2023) with High CAGR at 4%: MRFR," news release, February 2020, www.digitaljournal.com/pr/42 60757.

3. "Mars Petcare Builds Direct Relationships," WARC, March 8, 2018, www.warc.com/newsandopinion/news/mars_petcare_builds_direct_relationships/40149.

4. Pamela N. Danziger, "Pets Are Going Digital: The Brands Pioneering the $565 Million Market for Smart Pet Products," *Forbes*, January 30, 2019, www.forbes.com/sites/pamdanziger/2019/01/30/pets-are-going-digital-brands-pioneering-in-the-565m-market-for-smart-pet-products/#1932edad74b5.

5. Leonid Sudakov, "Mars Petcare on 21st Century Brand Connectivity," video, filmed at the 2018 IAB Annual Leadership Meeting, February 11–13, 2018, Palm Springs, CA, posted February 13, 2018, www.youtube.com/watch?v=j4Mvdmxaw6U&t=9s.

6. Stacey Higginbotham, "Goodbye Anki, Hello Connected Pets," *Internet of Things* (podcast), May 2, 2019, https://staceyoniot.com/podcast-goodbye-anki-hello-connected-pets/.

7. Higginbotham, "Goodbye Anki."

8. Higginbotham, "Goodbye Anki."

9. Sudakov, "Mars Petcare."

10. Gary Hamel and Michele Zanini, "The End of Bureaucracy," *Harvard Business Review*, November–December 2018.

11. Hamel and Zanini, "The End of Bureaucracy."

12. Hamel and Zanini, "The End of Bureaucracy," 53.

13. OECD, *An Introduction to Online Platforms and Their Role in the Digital Transformation* (Paris, France: OECD Publishing), https://read.oecd-ilibrary.org/science-and-technology/an-introduction-to-online-platforms-and-their-role-in-the-digital-transformation_bbaee7ce-en#page1.

14. Martin Reeves, "The Global Hunt for the Next Decade's Fastest-Growing Companies," *Fortune*, October, 18, 2018, https://fortune.com/2018/10/18/future-50-fastest-growing-companies/.

15. Melissa D. Curtis et al., "Development and Validation of a High-Quality Composite Real-World Mortality Endpoint," *Health Services Research* 53, no. 6 (December 2018), https://onlinelibrary.wiley.com/doi/full/10.1111/1475-6773.12872.

16. Jacqueline Corrigan-Curay, *Framework for FDA's Real-World Evidence Program* (Washington, DC: US Food and Drug Administration, 2019), 35, www.fda.gov/downloads/ScienceResearch/SpecialTopics/RealWorldEvidence/UCM627769.pdf.

17. "Innovation," Kloeckner Metals, https://www.kloecknermetals.com/the-kloeckner-advantage/innovation/.

18. Harvard Kennedy School Institute of Politics, "Clinton in Commanding Lead over Trump Among Young Voters, Harvard Youth Poll Finds," news release, April 25, 2016, https://iop.harvard.edu/youth-poll/past/harvard-iop-spring-2016-poll.

Conclusion: New Ways Forward

1. Kelly, "AR Will Spark"; Bruce Rogers, "Q&A with Rishad Tobaccowala: Staying Human in an Age of Data," *Forbes*, April 2, 2019.

2. Tanguy Catlin, Johannes-Tobias Lorenz, and Shannon Varney, "How Insurers Can Get the Most out of a Digital Transformation in 2018," *McKinsey Digital* (blog), February 23, 2018, www.mckinsey.com/business-functions/digital-mckinsey/our-insights/digital-blog/how-insurers-can-get-the-most-out-of-a-digital-transformation-in-2018.

3. Platform-Index, www.plattform-index.com/.

Index

Credit: Janusz Tomczyk

Erich Joachimsthaler is the founder and chief executive officer of Vivaldi Group, a leading global growth strategy firm that answers the complex brand and transformation questions that affect businesses today. He is the award-winning author of several books and over one hundred articles. He received his doctoral degree from the University of Kansas and was a postdoctoral fellow at Harvard Business School. He has received numerous awards and distinctions for his work, writing, and research. He is one of the most sought-after keynote speakers at industry conferences and company meetings. He lives in New York City.

Visit him online at www.erichjoachimsthaler.com.